DAME AGNES WESTON

DAME AGNES WESTON

by
Doris Gulliver

With a Foreword by
Admiral Sir Horace Law, K.C.B., O.B.E., D.S.C.

PHILLIMORE
London and Chichester

1971

Published by

PHILLIMORE & CO. LTD.
Shopwyke Hall, Chichester, Sussex, England

© Copyright — Doris Gulliver, 1971

All rights reserved

SBN 900592 27 3

Text composed by Phillimore in IBM 11/12pt. Press Roman
Printed by Eyre & Spottiswoode (Portsmouth) Ltd.,
at the Grosvenor Press

CONTENTS

Foreword	ix
Acknowledgments	xi
Chapter I	1
Chapter II	19
Chapter III	27
Chapter IV	38
Chapter V	51
Chapter VI	64
Chapter VII	78
Chapter VIII	93
Chapter IX	108
Chapter X	120
Chapter XI	130
Chapter XII	144
Bibliography	155
Index	157

LIST OF ILLUSTRATIONS

between pages

I	The young Agnes Weston at the beginning of her lifelong work	24 and 25
II	Agnes Weston and Sophia Wintz, co-founders of the Royal Sailors' Rests	
III	Agnes Weston, LL.D	
IV	Agnes Weston and Sophia Wintz	
V	Miss Weston visits a coastguard station	
VI	Miss Weston at the Royal Naval Barracks, Devonport	
VII	Joining the Royal Navy Temperance Society	72 and 73
VIII	Royal Sailors' Rest, Devonport, 1924	
IX	Royal Sailors' Rest, Portsmouth, 1915	
X	The Memorial Windows	
XI	Night School at the Portsmouth Rest	
XII	Home, Sweet Home	
XIII	A sailor's life	
XIV	My mother	
XV	Saying good-bye to 'Granny'	136 and 137
XVI	Jack's treasures	
XVII	A 'cabin', presented by Queen Victoria	
XVIII	Off duty on H.M.S. *Bonaventure*	
XIX	Royal Sailors' Rest, Devonport, after the blitz, 22 April 1941	
XX	Royal Sailors' Rest, Portsmouth, after the blitz, 10 January 1941	
XXI	Clearing the site of the Royal Sailors' Rest, Portsmouth	

FOREWORD

I am very honoured to have been asked to write a Foreword to this human and sensitive account of the life of Dame Agnes Weston.

Agnes Weston saw the Navy's needs of her time starkly and clearly, and she allowed nothing of her position or her sex to prevent her meeting those needs so far as she could. The obstacles in her path were formidable but she overcame them, relying entirely on her belief that she was doing God's work in the power of His Spirit.

In her work she did not have the advantages of modern means of publicity yet she was admired by, and was friends with, Kings and Queens, Admirals and ordinary seamen; and no matter how far her fame and influence spread in the Service she never lost the common touch, or the ability to see the needs of the sailor and his family.

This work is indeed a fitting tribute to so great a Lady and it will do all who read it good to know what can be done by God through the life of one faithful servant to alleviate the conditions and combat the evils of her time.

HORACE LAW

ACKNOWLEDGMENT

I should like to express my deep appreciation for all the help and encouragement I received from the staffs at the Agnes Weston House and the Royal Sailors' Rests at Portsmouth and Plymouth. Without their active co-operation I should have found the task of writing this book an extremely difficult one.

I also thank Mrs. C. Weston who allowed me to use letters, diaries and papers which are the property of the Weston family.

I acknowledge the courtesy of Mr. D. Jarrett for allowing me to quote from his book, *British Naval Dress*.

I

ON TWO of the many nights in 1941, when the holocaust was devastating Portsmouth and Devonport and the Royal Sailors' Rests in these two cities were destroyed, fifty years of the life's work of Dame Agnes Weston seemed to be in ruins. True, the buildings were razed, but bombs could not halt this work which had been built on the strongest foundation of all—that of Christian endeavour.

Who was Agnes Weston, who for half a century had been known to countless sailors as 'The Mother of the Navy', 'The Navy's Friend', 'The Lady of the Navy', or simply, but very lovingly, as 'Aggie'?

All these titles suited her well: it might be imagined that a woman so honoured by the Navy was born within the sight of the Sallyport or the Hoe; that her father was a bemedalled admiral, or that her mother's family was 'navy'. Nothing of the kind, she had no early connections with the Senior Service.

Her paternal grandfather, Samuel Weston, lived in Weymouth, where he was a prosperous merchant. He belonged to an old and honoured line and, according to the family saga, was a tall and extremely handsome man who died from typhus fever in the year of Waterloo. Of his family of thirteen children, the youngest, Charles Henry, became Agnes' father. Charles was born in 1802, and as a young man went to India where he hoped to become a partner in a firm in Madras. He did not stay there very long as he could not become accustomed to the heat and was never well. He therefore decided to come back to England, where he quickly recovered and enjoyed good health for many years afterwards. He gave up all idea of becoming a merchant and went to Trinity College, Cambridge, where he read law. He enjoyed Cambridge so much that for the rest of his life he remembered those happy days and dearly loved to talk of them to his family. While studying at Cambridge he met Agnes Bayly, and knew that she was the woman he wanted to marry. Her father, Judge Robert Bayly, a Bencher of Gray's Inn, gave his consent to the match with the proviso that before the marriage Charles Henry must be established as a barrister.

Robert Bayly was evidently a man of many accomplishments. From a family note, probably written by his grandson, we learn that the Judge was a man of high intelligence, great integrity, and devoted to hard mental study. His memory was above average and of exceptional retentive power, not only on matters in his own profession but over a wide diversity of subjects. He was a gifted conversationalist who enjoyed an attentive audience. Although quick tempered he kept himself well under control. In appearance he was of medium height with a good carriage and a very fine forehead. He was a judge on the Western Circuit, and when he travelled he would be accompanied by his wife, Anne, and one of his daughters. These ladies were always treated most courteously, and parties, balls and other entertainments were arranged for their enjoyment. When Agnes Bayly accompanied her father she doubtless found this social life very exciting, but her great inclination was to work for the betterment of the poor and needy. 'Slumming', as it was disparagingly called, was not countenanced by the parents and guardians of well brought-up young girls in the reign of George III. Her transport in London was a sedan chair and her chaperon a liveried footman. To undertake any form of social work in the slums of London thus attended would have been very difficult. She saw much change during her life: when she was young there was no gas, no railways, no police force, and all the ships in the navy were wooden vessels.

Charles Weston, eager to fulfil Judge Bayly's condition for marriage, worked so hard for his degree that his eyesight suffered and towards his finals he had to employ a reader, but despite this disability he passed with honours. After his examinations his sight improved, and he had no more trouble with it. He described

Chapter I

himself as the modern Jacob, but apart from the long period of waiting for his bride there seems to have been no other similarity.

The young couple were eventually married in 1836, just after the death of William IV, and before the coronation of Victoria during whose lifetime Britain changed so greatly. The Westons settled in Great Coran Street, described by the young Mr. Weston as a hive of barristers. In those days the strict hierarchy of the legal profession was maintained outside as well as inside the Courts. In the imposing squares, Queen's, Tavistock and Russell, lived the exclusive coterie of judges, for even in those days to maintain a household in the Squares needed a substantial bank balance. In the streets which led from these Squares lived the more wealthy barristers, whilst on the periphery of Bloomsbury the less successful members of the Inns of Court existed.

Charles and Agnes were idyllicly happy, and their children came in quick succession but, like those in so many Victorian families, only a few survived of those born. In her early years Agnes had experienced the sorrow of death in the home and saw the anguish of her own mother who lost several daughters with tuberculosis despite the care with which she nursed them. She would never trust her sick children to the untrained professional nurses of the time. So devoted was Anne Bayly to her patient that even when pregnant she continued to sleep, not only in the same room, but in the same bed as a fifteen year-old consumptive daughter so that if she woke in the night she would find her mother there to comfort her.

The Westons' first two sons died as babies, and later they lost a cherished little boy, who lived to be five and a half. Charles and Agnes were more fortunate than many, for three of their family survived and reached old age. These were Agnes (a family name of the Westons and the Baylys), Emily and Charles. Agnes was born on 28 March 1840, the year Victoria and Albert were married, and she never tired of hearing her mother tell of the celebrations for the coronation and the wedding which rocked the whole of London.

Frequent childbirth and tragic loss caused Mrs. Weston's health to fail, and it was unanimously decided by the doctors attending her that it was not desirable for her to continue to live in London. After much thought the family planned to move to Bath. This city had quietened since Jane Austen's time, but it was still beautiful, and will remain so whilst the Georgian buildings and the elegant Nash terraces stand. In 1845 Bath was no longer the centre of fashion it had been in the 18th century. Sea bathing, although still much restricted (especially for women), had largely replaced the taking of the waters of the inland spas. Perhaps it was George IV's interest in Brighton that caused the aristocracy to move from Bath to Brighton for their pleasure, or perhaps it was the latter's nearness to London which made it the new playground of the rich and their satellites. The Westons, however, were not seeking high society: their need was clean air and a quiet life. Agnes said that she remembered being taken to Paddington Station, going on one of those 'new fangled arrangements the railway', and on reaching Bath, being taken to her new home, Sion Place on Lansdown. The journey made such an impression on her that although she was not quite six when it happened, she declared that she never forgot it. All her life she found London vital and exciting, but when in later years she returned to Bloomsbury, and saw that her grandfather's home had been bought for a hotel and her former home had become a rather run-down boarding house, she had no wish to visit that district again.

At her Bath home the lawns and trees delighted her, as did the surrounding countryside. The Westons were a happy household, for nothing gave Mr. Weston more satisfaction than to share his pleasures with his children. He had never been the typical reserved Victorian father, for even as a barrister he would hurry back from the Courts to romp with his young daughter, and he used to say that was the best part of the whole day. Away from the discipline of his legal work he was deeply contented for he had time to follow his interests. He studied astronomy and had a telescope erected in the garden. He later became a Fellow of the Royal Astronomical Society. Naturally the telescope interested all the family, none more so than Agnes who had an enquiring mind which prompted her to find out things for herself. Father and daughter spent nights studying the infinite intricacies of the stellar universe. Clergymen today sometimes blame the emptiness of their churches on the teaching of science—especially space research—which makes some doubt the existence of God. The study of the universe had no such effect on Mr. Weston: 'All this,' he would declare, 'was created by God, every speck in the sky is part of the wonderful universe He has made for us.'

Mr. Weston's other great love was geology. In 1850 such studies as astronomy and geology were uncommon except for declared scientists, and his neighbours were often astonished to see Agnes and her father trudging home with a large basket of what seemed to be mere stones but which were valuable specimens to these amateur geologists. Together they would identify each item, label and exhibit it in the home museum. Mrs. Weston's pastimes of painting and literature were more tranquil. In such a home Agnes' education was much wider than that of most girls in the same social class. It has been often stated by educationalists, even by the early Greek philosophers, that the real mental development of a child depends on the influence of the parents in the home, learning in school being complementary. Although this dictum has been largely disregarded and emphasis placed on the school with home taking second place, there are signs in recent official reports that the advice of the ancient educationalists is at last being heeded. We read in the family journal that 'Agnes enjoyed neat advantages in early life both of her parents giving her every educational advantage, and also from the close companionship of her father and the friends who collected around him'. With her formal schooling she seemed neither impressed nor depressed; admittedly when she went to her first school she, usually so quick in her movements, declared that like Shakespeare's schoolboy she crept like a snail unwillingly to school. Agnes found the lessons monotonous with no kind of activity to relieve the drudgery of repetitive work. How different, she says, from the kindergartens she saw later in her life.

At about twelve years of age she was sent to an Academy for young ladies in Somerset Place. This was much better than her earlier school, but during all the time she was there her red-letter days were the Sundays spent at home. Marriage was the goal of most young women at that time and training was channelled towards that end. Organised games for girls were rare, and certainly not practised at Somerset Place where recreation took the form of gentle walks in the garden or stately formal dancing. For girls as energetic as Agnes, and there must have been many, such a life was frustrating. Her chief delight was essay writing, and in this she found an outlet for creative ability, although in a way not intended by the compiler of the school curriculum. In the top form, where there were nine pupils, each girl had to write a weekly essay, and for practice in enunciation had to read the composition aloud. For those lacking in imagination or too lazy to write at length, this was a task indeed, but to Agnes it was a joy. Weekly she wrote all the nine essays, thus employing herself happily, while gaining the gratitude of her fellow students, and at the same time satisfying the teacher. Literature studies at Somerset Academy were doled out purely as a form of punishment; for various misdeeds the exquisite lines of Shakespeare, or the noble stanzas of Milton, were written in copperplate handwriting and learnt by heart for subsequent recitation to a bored teacher. What crimes have been committed to ensure 'just punishment'.

When she left school Agnes was far less robust than was thought desirable; her father was concerned about her as he had always considered her a very fit young person. Encouraged to take up swimming and riding, she found these exercises exhilarating and was thrilled by her riding clothes which she describes in detail. She describes how dressed in her habit, her beaver hat with a large feather in it, and carrying her crop she felt most elegant. This was an unusual admission for Agnes, for all her life she had little interest in clothes, especially those for herself. She enjoyed these new activities, as she enjoyed everything else at this stage of her life, but all the time she was aware of an inner tumult. Apart from the general feeling of inadequacy which any thinking woman doubtless experienced in that era of massive male domination, Agnes must have been conscious that she was at the end of a line noted for its longevity and service to the country.

The first known member of the family was Reginald de Raoul de Bailleul, who fought so courageously for Duke William's cause that he was rewarded from the spoils of war with land and property. In addition he was created Viscount of Shrewsbury. Later he married Aimeria, niece and adopted daughter of the Earl of Shrewsbury. Everything prospered for the Viscount, he was given additional manors, Weston, Barton, Bruton and Newton, and his marriage brought him many additional estates. He had no wish to return to Normandy to control his French interests, and so that duty fell to his eldest son, who unfortunately for him, backed

Chapter I

Duke Robert to snatch the English crown, and when defeated had to flee for his life. He joined the crusaders, and in the meanwhile the castle in Normandy was burnt and the lands plundered.

As the eldest son was unable to return to England for fear of execution the second son, Hugo de Bailleul de Weston succeeded, on his father's death, to all the English lands.

Then followed two courageous crusaders of whom Agnes was inordinately proud. The first, Sir Hamo de Weston, whose bravery was legendary, fought side by side with Richard Coeur de Lion. The second, Hugh de Weston, many years later, fought a hand to hand combat with a Saracen standard bearer, killed his opponent and wrested the standard from the dying man. For Hugh's bravery Prince Edward added to the Weston crest of an eagle, a Saracen's head with his death cry, 'I am spent'.

A favourite ancestor of the Westons was Robert Weston, Lord Chancellor of Ireland in the days of Queen Elizabeth I, because he was a sincere worker and a good earnest Christian. Agnes says, 'We never know how far a good man's prayers may travel to his successors'. Was she thinking that such prayers could have travelled to her?

Another important man in the family tree was Richard Weston, created Earl of Portland by James I, but seems to have been equally favoured by Charles I, who made him Governor of the Isle of Wight, and Lieutenant-Governor of Southampton. The title died when his grandson, Charles, was killed in a naval battle against the Dutch in 1665, and it was not revived until William III reintroduced it, and from thence the Earls of Portland have played a memorable role in the history of this country. Mr. Weston used to say that any vitality in the old stock should be used for God and for good. We note with what pride he said this.

Agnes was fascinated by the past but found it no answer to her search for a full life. Her parents prayed for her for they were secretly worried about their daughter and did not know where her desires would lead as at that time she had no place in her life for religion. Charles and his wife were practising Christians, and had declared themselves so during their engagement when they had been so moved by the Reverend Baptist Noel, the Billy Graham of the time. They knew the solace their faith had given them in times of sorrow and because of this they tried to persuade Agnes at least to listen to their message, but she deliberately shut religion out of her life. At that time, perhaps because of the prevalent Victorian desire to force a ready-made faith on everyone, Agnes, a very independent character, refused to have any dogma thrust upon her. Whatever the reasons were, she says herself she did not want to be religious, it was as simple as that. There must have been a thinking minority who saw that it was not religion, but the church of the time that was unsound if not suspect. A contemporary note in her diary reflects her opinion that church-going was 90 per cent hypocrisy and 10 per cent sincerity. She watched her friends being confirmed, not because they wished to renounce the devil and all his ways, but because they wanted to attend the Easter Ball. In her friends' homes she must have seen the gulf between the 'haves' with their full and pleasant lives and the 'have nots', the maids working twelve hours a day for a mere pittance while shop assistants were pale and under-nourished because of their low wages. Agnes wondered what part the Church was playing in improving conditions for the under-privileged.

The churches were full in those days because it was the expected thing for people to go regularly to Matins or Evensong. While employers filled their family pews domestics, suitably hatted and gloved, worshipped from the benches at the back of the House of God, having already performed their household tasks. It was a nice, cosy time for the local vicar, when hand-shakes and tea parties were often a substitute for the hard lesson of a compelling Gospel. When the Reverend James Fleming came to All Saints' Church in Bath the congregation found he was not one who could shut his eyes to what was wrong, nor could he take the easy road. He had a burning desire to act as Christ would have him act, and fortunately for Agnes, and subsequently for thousands of others, James Fleming gained her confidence and trust. At first when he preached she was determined not to listen, insisting that he had nothing to tell her. Often if she could not distract her thoughts, she would cover up her ears, and think 'You go on, you shan't have my attention, I can't hear what you're saying'. Or during the sermon she would read a novel. In this she was like the Quaker reformer, Elizabeth Fry, who did everything she could to escape from concentrating on the message; she said that she counted the eyelets in her boots over and over again to

Chapter I

avoid listening. But in early womanhood when Elizabeth heard the famous American preacher William Savery, nothing could prevent her from receiving the Gospel; she became a devout believer, and the world was to know the great work she did to help the women prisoners of this country, and how penal reformers throughout Europe copied her methods.

Miss Weston was being watched, and because the Reverend James Fleming was a born psychologist, much more important than to be just a trained one, he judged the right time to talk to her as a responsible adult. He ignored her flippant attitude towards him and all that he said, and begged her to consider confirmation. Then, as if this had been the moment she had been waiting for, she poured out her difficulties and doubts. He listened with understanding. but offered no advice. Gradually, however, he gained her complete confidence. He did this without obviously seeking it, and never attempted to press her into doing something which she considered dishonest. Carefully, step by step, he guided her to an understanding of the Gospel. Slowly she began to accept her faith and when she was prepared to take Christ as her Guide, she consented to be confirmed and never again did she have one moment's doubt in her trust in God. The Reverend James Fleming later became rector of St. Michael's Church in Chester Square, London, where week after week he talked from his pulpit to the cream of London aristocracy. They praised him for his preaching and guidance, but all the praise he received did not alter him and to the end of his life he remained the humble priest seeking to help the unsure and the disbeliever as Christ had bade him do.

He had a profound effect on Agnes; he had shown her the way to a spiritual peace, and became her mentor until the end of his life. She was determined to make her religion live, but what did Christ want her to do? That she did not know; what she did know was that He did not want her to lead a frivolous life of balls and receptions, punctuated with mild flirtations. For her answer she had to wait.

Just at this time her father decided to move, and he planned a beautiful family house to be built at the top of Lansdown Hill, on a site 700 feet above sea level. Such a position would be especially healthy for his family and particularly beneficial for his wife. She had spent two years in her own room at Sion Place, and the state of her health was causing concern. Fortunately her husband's hopes were fulfilled and after being for sometime confined to her room in the new house she was eventually able to get out in the grounds of her lovely home and, although never strong, lived there in great happiness for many years.

But we have raced ahead, for the house took some months to design and with these plans Agnes was her father's chief and most enthusiastic helper. When completed the house was called 'Ensleigh', because it was at the end of the lea. The gardens were laid out by Sir Joseph Paxton, and comprised extensive lawns, flower beds, a useful kitchen garden and a magnificent fernery. A croquet lawn was included for the game, which was to sweep over England, was then just becoming popular, although it was still considered a little bold for young women to play it. In the grounds, there were large conservatories, a stable, and a carefully erected observatory to house Mr. Weston's latest acquisition, a nine-inch telescope. In addition there was built a small museum, quite separate from the house, for the geological specimens.

The land outside 'Ensleigh' drops suddenly and the Westons had a glorious panoramic view across the chalk downs of Wiltshire to the old city of Bath. How pleasant this must have been for Mrs. Weston, who could seldom journey far. For the rest of the family the hill must have been rather a strain in bad weather and Agnes says that often in winter she slipped down long tracts of it; but for all that she loved the place which was her home whenever she liked to stay there until her mother's death in 1895.

After they were installed at 'Ensleigh', Agnes went on a visit to the home of her uncle, Charles Fox, in Plymouth. He was devoted to music and an expert musician, especially accomplished on the organ. In his music room he had a fine chamber organ, with some twenty stops and two and a half octaves of pedals. When her uncle played Agnes was overwhelmed by the magnificence of it; it did not sound like one instrument, but filled the whole room as a full orchestra might have done. Charles Fox could tell her interest was no passing fancy and set about teaching her the rudiments of organ music; when she returned to Lansdown she studied under Mr. J.K. Pyne, organist at the Abbey Church, Bath. As usual she worked with all her might, practising so hard that often the boy blowing the organ was exhausted, and Agnes had to stop to let

Chapter I

him rest. Her progress was good, and Mr. Pyne suggested that Dr. Wesley, organist at Gloucester Cathedral, might possibly accept her as a pupil. The Doctor was loth to consider an amateur as a pupil, and a woman amateur at that! But Mr. Pyne prevailed on him, and eventually the Doctor said that he would give her a trial; he made no promises and would only take her on if she showed exceptional talent, although he could not imagine a woman organist doing that.

So that she should not have any false hopes of playing in the Cathedral Dr. Wesley did not invite her to Gloucester, but suggested that she should meet and play for him at Cheltenham parish church. Agnes arrived early. She went to view the organ and finding the blower ready, sat down and began to play. She rehearsed several pieces and then went on to one of her favourites, Bach's Fugue in G minor. In the meanwhile Dr. Wesley who had crept into the church, sat down at the back and listened; he was unprepared for her technique and was filled with admiration at what he heard. He accepted her as a pupil saying, 'I shall teach you as if you were going to be a professional. It'll be hard going, think you can stand it?' Agnes was sure she could, and had he known more of her pertinacity he would have known that she would go right on to the end of any task however difficult it became; this he was only to appreciate later. It seems strange to us that there was such secrecy over their meeting, and shows how reluctant men were to accept a woman into what was then considered a man's world.

Dr. Wesley had so much influence in the Cathedral that he had no difficulty in gaining permission for Miss Weston to play the organ. To play Bach and other masters of organ music in that truly magnificent cathedral, built in Norman time, stately and austere, must have been a memorable experience.

Agnes worked hard, practising not less than five hours a day, and says that it was agony for her master to have to endure a wrong note. As well as the joy she got from her own playing she gained inspiration from listening to Dr. Wesley. According to Mendelssohn, he was the greatest organist the world had known or was ever likely to know. He was so uplifted when he was playing that he inspired the congregation to sing as though their very hearts were in the words.

Sometimes at the end of the service he would play the people out with music from Handel, for he knew many of Handel's works from memory, but so lovely was his rendering of the piece that the congregation would remain to listen quite enraptured until the final clash of chords. At other times Dr. Wesley would finish with a work of his own, composing it as he went along; those fortunate enough to hear this music little realised that it was quite impromptu, and would never be repeated—they had indeed been the privileged few.

Dr. Wesley forgave Agnes both for being an amateur and a woman and sent Mr. Weston an excellent report of his daughter's ability. Mr. Weston felt that her talents should not be wasted, and bought her a chamber organ, which he had installed in the music room. This instrument gave her much pleasure for many years, both at home and later when it was moved to the centre of her work at Devonport.

When she left Gloucester to settle at 'Ensleigh' Agnes did not continue to attend All Saints' church, for the Reverend James Fleming had moved to London and also it was no longer her parish church. She went to St. Stephen's church which was pastored by the Reverend Philip Eliot, a young and excellent preacher. Above all he wanted to do good in his parish. He longed for his whole congregation to be as one big family with those who were able, ready and eager to help others in need. After only one attendance at the church, the vicar asked Miss Weston if she would teach in the Sunday School. She was a little diffident about attempting this, for she was unused to children, but said that she would be willing to try if she could be given the younger children; after the first lesson she found that not only had the class enjoyed the lesson, but so had she herself. The vicar supervised the whole Sunday School by visiting each group in turn; he soon realised that she would be able to manage the older children admirably and was confident that she could undertake his 'unruly' class of boys for whom he had been unable to find a suitable teacher.

When he asked her to take on this group, Agnes accepted the challenge, and as the months passed by it proved a very successful partnership. With her 'boys' (she refused to let them be called 'unmanageables') she made instant rapport. She did not try to 'get them down' but rather 'lift them up'. She found how interesting these lads could be: they were vital, alive, eager to learn and help. These were boys who found it difficult to submit to suppressive authority. We have plenty of young people now similar to those in Miss Weston's class. Today they march, they protest, they have 'sit-ins' and 'stay-outs' but in the 19th century the voice of youth, especially the poorer youth, was ignored or suppressed. The class continued better than she had ever dared to hope. She was delighted, and the vicar, no doubt, most relieved. But what more could she do? She was a dedicated Christian waiting to take on more and more Christian work. Her motto, after her confirmation, was a simple one with a wealth of meaning, 'Do ye the nexte thynge'. It is an Anglo-Saxon saying from which we presume that when one task has been completed or well established the doer should be ready to take on further work.

It certainly was so with Agnes: her next thing was to visit the patients in Bath United Hospital. She was invited by the Reverend E.J. Wright to talk to the sick and injured, and Agnes was honoured to have this opportunity of work which showed her pain and suffering as she had never seen it before; it proved to her that implicit faith is the only help that can be given to the dying. The experience she gained, bitter though it often was, proved of inestimable value in her later work. She prepared carefully for her visits, learning as much as she could about each patient so that she could communicate easily. She was able to greet each man by name and, from the abundance of the 'Ensleigh' gardens, to give each patient a present of fruit or flowers. Often she would put a New Testament on the locker beside the sick man's bed and then would pray with him. This was of ineffable value to a diseased or injured man, for here was a well-educated young woman, obviously of the upper classes, speaking to him as an equal and inviting him to share in her belief in Jesus Christ. Such conduct must have made a great impression on the patient. She became such a popular visitor that she was invited to give a short Gospel address in each ward every week and many who engage in social work in the 1970s would do well to consider and learn from Miss Weston's attitude to the poor and needy a century before.

While visiting the sick in Bath Hospital Agnes learnt of the work of Catherine Marsh. Some of the men talked to her of Miss Marsh's humanity and of her efforts to improve the conditions of living for the navy. When Agnes read Miss Marsh's works and learnt more of her campaign she was inspired and considered her a true pioneer of women's work; years after, when Catherine Marsh was very old, they corresponded, but they never met.

Gradually Agnes found that her social work absorbed more and more of her time and thoughts. Her first 'unmanageables' were now too old for Sunday School, but asked her to continue to lead them by forming a club. There were all kinds of difficulties, not the least of which was to find a meeting place. At first the meetings were held in the vestry of St. Stephen's church but the membership increased so fast that other accommodation had to be found. She was able to use the local schoolroom after school hours and this proved most suitable. Her 'boys' brought along friends, many of whom were married, and Agnes, ever a strong believer in family life, invited the wives to share in the happy meetings. Naturally the young women were only too pleased to participate and soon the schoolroom became inadequate. Then with Mr. Weston's help they moved the club to a Mission room in East Walcot. He paid for the hire of the premises—the members did everything else to make the hall attractive. It was cleaned and painted, brightened in every way possible until it became an attractive warm meeting hall for the group. It proved most popular, and as the membership increased different meetings had to be held on separate nights. Regularly each week there were Bible readings and Prayer meetings, and occasionally there would be social evenings.

Her work was spreading and her next task ultimately led Agnes to her life's work. The second Somerset Militia held their annual training at Bath. The officers were well catered for but it seems that little preparation was made for the comfort of the men; in this era rankers were not considered to be of any account in peacetime, although lauded in time of war when ample cannon fodder was of prime importance. During the training period in Bath there were no prepared camps or previously inspected lodgings for the men, who were mostly billeted in public houses. This, on the whole, was most unsatisfactory, for there was nowhere except the bar for the men to congregate after the day's exercise. One of the local clergy, the Reverend A.L. Dixon, became very concerned about this, and felt it was the duty of the

Chapter I

church to see that these men had proper recreation rooms. He asked Agnes for her help. She set about the job with her usual enthusiasm. First she found suitable premises—a disused shop; it was conveniently located and not expensive to rent. She fitted the largest room out as a coffee bar, with comfortable chairs, polished tables, charming curtains, and bright lights, in fact with every thing to make it a second home.

Naturally there was criticism from the many who did nothing of the few who did all. Miss Weston, they said, was trying to give the men ideas above their station. Mr. and Mrs. Weston were criticised for allowing their daughter so much liberty: it was unseemly for a young woman to be mixing with common soldiers—officers yes, but certainly not with ordinary privates. Fortunately the Westons were quite unperturbed by the malice which festered in drawing-rooms. As if to show their disdain Emily, Agnes' sister, also decided to give her full time services to the project.

The fitting out of such an establishment cost money, and after Agnes and Emily had contributed all they could afford, they collected from the people whom the Reverend A.L. Dixon had interested in the scheme. When still more money was needed Agnes went to ask the help of Colonel Pinney of Somerton, who was Colonel of the regiment and a great friend of her father, and the Colonel's sister, Lady Smith. Agnes found Lady Smith most generous; she was to interest herself in the work for many years.

The men greatly appreciated the comfort of the coffee-bar where they could enjoy home-made cakes, sandwiches, rolls and a variety of hot drinks. The refreshments were not free, for Agnes was convinced then, as she was during all her years with the services, that the men and their wives did not want charity. As soon as the first room was an established success Agnes and Emily opened a writing room, fitted with writing tables, stationery, pens, ink, and blotting paper. There were larger tables for games, racks full of newspapers and shelves of books. This room, to the men's delight, was equal to anything that could be found in the officers' mess. Sometimes there would be magic lantern shows and at other times dances were arranged. A third smaller room was opened for prayer meetings, Bible study and services, and used as the 'Quiet' room, something very precious and uncommon in the noisy communal life of a soldier. A harmonium was installed and Agnes Weston accompanied the hymn singing. So much was accomplished in one year, such a revolution in the amenities provided for the ranker; this work was to continue as long as the need was there, and Emily continued it after Agnes left Bath.

When the men went away many wrote to Agnes, mostly to thank her for all that had been done for them, but some of the militia joined the regular army and gradually many were drafted overseas. The thought of years of separation from England was very depressing for those whose parents and friends were illiterate because the soldiers knew that communication between them and home would be limited. They asked Agnes Weston if she would send them the news of England and she said she would do this willingly. Often the young red-coat was so dejected that he would write and ask for her prayers to help him through the strain of the parting. To these men she would write understanding and sympathetic answers; she told one lad that she could be as near to him in Calcutta as in Aldershot through a regular series of letters, and urged him not to despair.

On rainy days she spent the whole time at 'Ensleigh', writing to the soldiers who awaited letters from her or answering the letters of others. Their letters gave her an insight into places she would never visit and told her of people she would never see, while hers gave them local and national news, bright and cheerful tidings and comforting as well as challenging words from the Gospel—she was their link with home. Soon she was known throughout the country for her tireless letter-writing and was asked by the secretary of the Carus Wilson's Society for the Welfare of the Soldier if she would correspond with some of the Christian members of their Society. Willingly she consented—it was no task for her, she really enjoyed the work.

One letter she wrote to a young soldier while he was waiting in Portsmouth to sail to India seems to have been inspired. He read it over and over again; it was his one tie with home. Far out to sea he could keep his prized possession to himself no longer and showed it to a sick-berth attendant, George Brown, who rather enviously asked the soldier if he thought Miss Weston would send a letter to a lonely sailor. Tommy said he was sure that as she wrote to a 'red-coat' she would be equally ready to write to a 'blue-jacket',

Chapter I

and that he would send her George Brown's name to put on her mailing list. When she sent her letter to George Brown, sick-berth attendant of H.M.S. *Crocodile,* Agnes made her first contact with the navy. Many years later Brown told her how he had taken the letter to a quiet corner of the sick-bay so that he could read it in peace, and that he was so happy to receive it and so touched by the Christian message it contained he had wept unashamedly. Unable to keep it to himself he had shared it with his mates who begged him to ask the lady to write to them.

All through her life whatever Agnes Weston did had very small beginnings, but these branched to become an enormous tree. This was so with the letters: what began with a few letters to the men of the Somerset Militia finished with the monthly distribution of 55,000 letters. As the demand grew Agnes decided that she would have to supplement the written letter by a printed one, but during nearly half the century that she despatched these letters she never dictated one or missed a month, not even when on holiday or in hospital. When, in her own words, she was 'strung up' in Portsmouth hospital with a fractured leg and awkward as it was to write, she would not let anyone else do it for her. 'I always feel that while the men care to read my letters they should come right from my heart and go, I hope, to theirs,' was her reply to those eager to give assistance.

The replies she received from the men gave her both pleasure and pain. One man wrote, 'Ma'm we think so much of your letters, and we never even use them to light our pipes with'. This was praise indeed. Sometimes, a man unable to write would pay a writer to send an answer to Miss Weston, but she never had a joint letter such as two wives, Susan and Polly had, whose husbands, unable to pay the shilling charged by the professional writer, paid 6d. each so that their wives would know they were well. Miss Weston noted that after the turn of the 20th century the employment of the paid writer gradually ceased and thought that possibly the increase of education was slowly having its effect.

Sometimes the men to whom she wrote never returned; one very sad case was that of a rating with whom she had been corresponding for a long time. His excitement at coming home knew no bounds but just before he was due to return he was drafted to another ship. He was bitterly disappointed, but there was nothing he could do; he went on to tell Miss Weston that as he was sick and unwell, he thought perhaps it was because he was so miserable. When she received his very sad letter she wrote at once. He never received her answer, and months later she had it returned stamped 'DEAD'.

When H.M.S. *Alert* and H.M.S. *Discovery,* were detailed for an Arctic expedition, the crews were worried about the delivery of their monthly letters, known as the 'blue-backs'. Quite undaunted, Agnes wrote the thirty-six required for the following three years. These were put up in monthly batches and made watertight in large tin-lined tea chests. When the men returned they told her these 'blue-backs' were their only link with home in those cold dark waters.

In 1873 the young sailor boys under training asked for a letter just for themselves; she immediately complied with their wish and in the first month sent out over 500 copies. This letter too was written personally for the next forty-five years.

By that year some of the men to whom Agnes had first written were returning from their overseas duty, and begged her to go to Portsmouth and Devonport to meet them personally. To go to Portsmouth she felt was out of the question, but she looked forward to meeting some of her correspondents in Devonport, which was not too far from Bath; she knew that she would be welcome to stay with her aunt and uncle in Plymouth. Just as she was ready to go she received an invitation to speak to a party of naval wives, and the writer said that she would be honoured if Miss Weston would be her guest during her stay in Devonport. Agnes sent off a hasty note to say that she would be pleased to address the women, but that she would be staying with relations in Plymouth. When she left 'Ensleigh' and made her way to meet the ladies at Stoke, Devonport, she little realised that the "nexte great thynge" in her life was to begin.

II

IMAGINE AGNES' surprise when she was ushered into a charming drawing-room to be welcomed by a pretty fair-haired young woman who introduced herself as Sophia Wintz. Agnes knew that she had seen her before but at first she could not remember where. Then, suddenly, the picture became clear: it had been at a meeting for the study of prophecy in Bath during the previous Autumn. The room had been crowded and there had been no opportunity for Agnes to speak to the young woman. Mr. Weston had an appointment to keep directly the meeting closed, and he and Agnes had been forced to hurry away.

Now the two women had met again and were to become life-long friends and co-workers. This second meeting, and the almost immediate realisation that they had work to do together seems almost too much of a coincidence and, had it been written in a novel or a play, the writer would have been ridiculed for believing his readers to be so credulous. But this was not fiction: it was real life. The partnership that began on that afternoon was perfect. Twenty years later the Duke of Saxe Coburg said to them, 'It is splendid to see two women rowing in one boat all these years and not capsizing her'. I have asked many people, who knew them both, how it was that they not only remained good friends for nearly fifty years, but worked in harmony all that time and accomplished so much. The answer is always to the same effect, 'They had a great respect for each other as they had for all people, and of course each did her own work and never interfered with the other's work'.

Sophia Wintz's early life might almost have been written by Hans Andersen—it was a fairy-tale youth. Like her friend's, her ancestry was ancient, for we first read of the family in 1315 when Berchtold de Winze fought at Morgarten, against the Austrians, with disastrous results.

At the end of the 18th century John Conrad Wintz married Marie Magdalene de Wald-Kirch, a woman described as being of noble birth and of great beauty. Of their lives we know little, but their son Augustus was evidently an extraordinary man. He was a sound administrator and a good business man. In his district he was most highly esteemed and became president of his canton. The way he met his future wife was unusual. He saw a young woman who was holidaying with her aunt in Switzerland, and although he knew nothing about the English girl he fell desperately in love with her and vowed he would marry her. After her vacation she returned home, and speedily Augustus followed. He found where she lived, went to stay nearby, became friendly with her family, and finally persuaded the woman to marry him. She returned to Switzerland as his wife, and the mistress of Wintzenaue Castle. His mother, by that time a widow, moved into the dower house where she remained for many years.

Brief their courtship may have been, but the marriage was a very happy one. They had a family of six, two boys and four girls who must have been reared in near perfect surroundings. In their early years they were allowed to run wild in the extensive château lands. Round the castle were the formal continental gardens backed by extensive orchards from which, for miles, stretched the Wintz vineyards, among the most luxuriant in Switzerland. Behind the vineyards, like a majestic back-cloth, rose the snow-tipped mountains and all day the rush of the Falls of Schaffhausen could be heard.

The youngest but one of the Wintz children, Sophia Gertrude, was born with a sunny nature. Lessons were no worry to her. She had an English governess who saw that she learnt to speak and write English; apart from that Sophia's life was without restraint. When she was about eight, however, everything changed. Her eldest brother went to Heidelberg University and the father took the family to stay in that marvellous old city. Sophia was one of those people who as a child, or an adult, could adapt herself to her environment. When in Switzerland she played the games of a Swiss child and was as one of the local children; in Germany she played with the German children and lived her life as they did. Later when she came to England, she became just another English girl. She possessed the wonderful gift of being able to identify herself with the ambient life at any time or place—no regrets, comparisons or aloofness. This happy and unusual gift perhaps accounts for Sophia's popularity. Her brother was a brilliant university scholar and no doubt would have carved for himself a worthy career to be followed until he inherited the Château, but this was not to be. He caught a fever and in a few weeks was dead. Naturally the parents were grief stricken: the loss was so sudden, the blow so great. Frau Wintz felt that she could not return immediately to Schaffhausen where every stone of the place would remind her of her son; the only place where she felt she could find any consolation was in her native land. So they came back to England. It says much for the love and understanding of her husband that he let his wife spend the rest of her life in this country and never demanded that she should return to Switzerland. He spent part of the year on his estates on the continent, and the remainder with his family in England. When he died the Château and its lands were sold. It was not until 1885 that Sophia revisited her former home when she and Agnes went there for a holiday. They were treated like royalty. The hotel staff, the gardeners, the ferryman were all honoured to see one of the old family return, and in fact the ferryman refused to allow the visitors to pay, saying that the Wintz family had given his family the right to ferry under the Falls, so how could he take Miss Wintz's money?

This was only the second time that Agnes had been abroad: the first occasion was in 1871 when four members of her family had been invited by her Uncle Bayly to go to France and Italy. It is evident from her description of that tour that to be taken from one beauty spot to another, being waited on hand and foot, and to gaze at pictures and other man-made masterpieces was not sufficient for Agnes. Throughout her life she preferred to do things herself and to obtain a desired end through her own exertions rather than to be a spectator. She probably enjoyed herself very much more in 1876 when she and Sophia went for a holiday to Snowdon where they tramped and climbed in the glorious natural beauty of Wales.

When the Wintz family left Germany to settle in England they bought a large rambling house on Clarence Parade in Southsea. It had a magnificent view of the open sea, across Spithead and in the distance the Isle of Wight. Portsmouth and Southsea once were separate towns, just as Plymouth, Devonport and Stoke were separate until they were joined under the corporate name of Plymouth. Portsmouth had always been an interesting city, full of life and movement, and the drama of its history must be unsurpassed. As a town it is important, certainly vital, but never beautiful. Even the Romans passed it by and sailed up the creek to Portchester where they settled and built a castle, believing the now famous Portsmouth harbour to be useless. For many years Portchester continued to be of paramount importance, and as late as the 15th century it was used by Henry V as a place of embarkation for the expedition to France which culminated in the famous victory of Agincourt in 1415.

It seems extraordinary that Frau Wintz and her family could have tolerated the confined life at Southsea after all the magnificence of their Swiss estate. Southsea was then an area almost exclusively of homes for half-pay officers, boarding houses and hotels. Palmerston Road, one of the main thoroughfares, was entirely residential, with family houses standing back in very well laid-out gardens; Kings Road, then Wish Street, was also residential. Both these important roads have been transformed twice since then; in the beginning of the 20th century, they gradually became shopping centres and, from the early nineteen-forties they were areas of devastation for a decade. Now Kings Road has become mainly residential again while Palmerston Road is one of the principal shopping centres of the city, the shops being larger and more magnificent than those of the former era. The nearest open space that the Wintz children had to play on was Southsea Common, not the well-groomed garden of today but a tract of wild swampy gorse-ridden waste. Sophia seemed to be quite content. She and her brother played cricket there and with their neighbours formed a team which inevitably always batted on a very sticky wicket!

When her brother went as a naval cadet to the *Britannia,* Sophia went to school. Years later this brother became an admiral; Sophia

Chapter II

was inordinately proud of him and felt she could bask in his glory, like Jane Austen who declared 'Everyone will remember me for I have two brothers who are Admirals'. Both Jane and Sophia are well remembered, but not because of their brothers: they had no need at all for reflected glory.

Sophia's school was at Fareham, a small market town about twelve miles from Southsea. To get there she drove in a carriage along the Commercial Road which was to become so familiar to her later, then almost at once into the country as the whole of the northern part of Portsmouth was farm land. Then she would go through Hilsea under the Arches, the old fortifications of Portsmouth, and over Port's Bridge, which until fairly recently was the only route in or out of the town, following the water's edge to Portchester and thence to Fareham. It was a day's outing from Clarence Parade to Fareham. Unlike most girls she thoroughly enjoyed boarding school; with her keen intelligent mind, ready sympathy, and capacity for making friends she was popular with staff and fellow pupils, besides which any girl who had travelled as extensively as she had and who had enjoyed such a romantic background must have caught the imagination of the other girls.

When she left school she enjoyed the luxurious life of a rich young woman. Like an Austen heroine she flitted from Bath to Weymouth, on to Clifton and thence to Plymouth, and then began the season's routine all over again, revelling in every minute of her life of balls, house-parties and race-meetings. She enjoyed all kinds of sports, and when staying on country estates she fished and rode and was considered by her many admirers to be an excellent horsewoman. Then, in the natural course of events, she became engaged. Her fiancé was an Army officer, and had she married him it is most likely she would have had a normal service married life, and lived and died unhonoured and unsung. Although marriage was the accepted thing for a girl of her position Sophia had doubts and felt unsure about taking this irrevocable step. She postponed the day of the ceremony and visited a friend at Temple Combe; where the atmosphere was almost that of a retreat. There she spent much time alone in prayer and contemplation; away from the gay frivolity of her circle she was conscious of a depth of thought of which she had not previously known herself capable. She prayed for guidance. Her prayers were answered. Before the time of her departure she knew that she must give to others, not only money, which is so easy to give but, much harder, she must give herself. She left Temple Combe a relieved young woman, for there is perhaps no greater mental strain than that of indecision, but once the resolution has been made then life seems to unburden as Christian found when he had struggled through the Slough of Despond. When Sophia reached home she broke off her engagement and prepared herself for a life of service. It was in the same year that this happened that she began her working partnership with Agnes Weston.

The two women were, in some ways, entirely different personalities: Sophia was very interested in clothes and from admiring descriptions we read of her charming appearance in lace-trimmed velvet gowns, fashionable hats and furs. The greatest interest that Agnes ever took in her clothes seemed to have been many years before she met Sophia when she was rigged out in her elegant riding habit. Sophia loved animals; for recreation her favourite day away from duty was spent at a zoo watching the antics of the animals, while her friend's similar interest seems to have been confined to her two dogs, a pony and a parrot. Sophia was more interested in the potential achievements of women than her friend, who concentrated on the everyday life of the sailor's mothers or wives. When eventually Sophia took over the running of the Rests and the editing of *Ashore and Afloat,* she made constant references to the success of women in the professional fields. These differences were unimportant as the common ground of their partnership was their strong conviction that they had been called by God to work for the good of the underprivileged, and to guide the lower ranks of the Royal Navy from their despond of drink and consequent degradation.

In 1873 in Plymouth alone nearly 4,000 boys were being trained for the Royal Navy. The training ships were H.M.S. *Implacable,* H.M.S. *Lion,* H.M.S. *Foudroyant* all of which were anchored in the Hamoaze. In addition to these lads in Plymouth, there were also a great number under training on the *St. Vincent* at Portsmouth; on H.M.S. *Ganges* at Falmouth, and H.M.S. *Boscawen* at Portland. The number of trainees today is considerably less, but in the last quarter of the 19th century the Navy was expanding rapidly and men were urgently needed. Nowadays the

II AGNES WESTON AND SOPHIA WINTZ, co-founders of the Royal Sailors' Rests

I THE YOUNG AGNES WESTON at the beginning of her lifelong work

III AGNES WESTON, LL.D

IV AGNES WESTON AND SOPHIA WINTZ

VI MISS WESTON at the Royal Naval Barracks, Devonport

V MISS WESTON VISITS A COASTGUARD STATION

Chapter II

young cadets are trained in shore bases but then the boys from the Plymouth ships were only allowed ashore on Sunday afternoons, and as Miss Wintz watched them wander up and down the main street for the whole afternoon, she became at first interested by their aimlessness, and then distressed that there really seemed nothing for them to do, and nowhere for them to go except into public houses. To enter these was forbidden, and even if the boys had felt inclined to break the rules their meagre pocket-money would have been quickly spent. If Miss Wintz had been born in the Midlands or the North of England this aimless sauntering would not have surprised her so much, for in many of the smaller towns it was a common sight to see a mass of young people strolling up and down the main street, rarely making new friends, creating no disturbance, and taking no interest even in other groups—just stretching their legs after a week in the mines or factories. This situation was unaltered until the Second World War when the cinemas were opened on Sundays, and more cafés and clubs were available to young people. Miss Wintz had never lived north of the Thames, and she felt that the local people should invite the naval lads to their homes and make them welcome. The fact that they were not part of the Devonport community worried her and she discussed the problem with Agnes who suggested that perhaps the best thing they could do would be to consult the boys' officers. These, with true naval conservatism, thought that the lads were all right and would prefer their liberty to being organised. Sophia agreed that this was probably true if it was a purely service arrangement, but surely the young men would like to meet some of the civilians of Devonport? The two women decided to persevere with their idea and hired the Mechanics' Hall in Devonport, a drab and uninviting place according to Miss Weston, who hoped free buns would attract the sailor boys—they didn't; and it seemed as if the officers were right, for the only lad who turned up for the initial opening fled when he saw he was alone. So it was for four successive Sundays, and it seemed as if the lads needed no help to provide them with entertainment during their off-duty hours. Then Mrs. Wintz, Sophia's mother, who was more experienced in the ways of nautical men (her son was under training, and her brother was Admiral Sir Lewis Jones, who lived to be over ninety and who was described by Edward VII as the doyen of the Navy) suggested that the boys wanted the warmth and comfort of a home and offered her kitchen which amply satisfied these conditions. This idea was welcomed by the younger women; a meeting was advertised for the following Sunday, when a fair-haired lad led a shy and diffident party into the welcoming warmth of Mrs. Wintz's kitchen. The leader was a boy named Arthur Phillips, already dedicated to Christian work. He was always present at the Sunday meetings until, when just over seventeen, he was transferred to H.M.S. *Triumph*. 'Just for six months,' he said, 'then I shall be back'—but he met with an accident on board the ship and died instantly. This tragic loss of one so promising deeply affected Miss Weston and Miss Wintz. But life has to go on whatever the sorrow, and the number of boys gathering in Mrs. Wintz's kitchen increased Sunday by Sunday until there was literally no room for any more. The meetings opened with enthusiastic hymn singing, then a reading from the Bible, and discussions followed by an address; refreshments were served and no doubt eaten with gusto by the young sailors.

These 'family' meetings continued for several years before Miss Weston's next venture provided larger accommodation. We can imagine with what curiosity, and indeed apprehension, the two good women watched the boys come and go, wondering how they would fare when they were no longer trainees but fully-fledged ratings in the Navy, with more freedom and more money to spend. The Britain of those days was not a hospitable place for the young sailor.

III

WHEN AGNES Weston began her work with the Navy far too many Britons were addicted to strong drink; every class, from the brandy-swilling aristocracy to the beer and gin-topers of the working classes, drank far more than was good for them.

In the Navy a liberal ration of rum (or tot as it was called) was considered necessary to keep the men healthy; whether this was so, or whether it was to placate the harsh life and meagre food allowances we do not know. In 1740 however, Admiral Vernon, affectionately called 'old Grog' because of the grogram boat-cloak which he wore, wrote home from Jamaica that there had been various desertions because the men were 'stupefied with Spiritous Liquors'. After he had discussed this problem with his medical officers and with his captains he decided that the daily ration of ½ pint of rum per man should be diluted with an equal measure of water. This was to be mixed in one scutteled butt kept for the purpose, and the mixing carried out by the officer of the watch. In 1825 this ration was cut down to a gill and to ½ a gill in 1850. Admiral Vernon was more popular with the men than with the Admiralty and in later life he was cashiered for his attacks on the Government. But those who dishonoured him have long since been forgotten whereas he has been remembered on two counts: first by the Naval torpedo school at Portsmouth, named H.M.S. *Vernon;* and secondly by the word 'grog' introduced into the English language.

Queen Victoria knew that sailors were served with rum for

when she inspected her fleet in 1842, she asked to taste the men's grog and declined it served in a delicate glass, demanding a pannikin just as the men had, and after a few sips declared it very good.

The many inn signs throughout the country bearing the names of our famous admirals, sea victories, or just *Jolly Jack, The Jovial Sailor* or *The Merry Tar* give the impression that hard drinking was confined to the Navy. On the contrary, for from the 18th to the 20th centuries drink was the greatest scourge since the plagues; it undermined the whole social life of the working classes which constituted the majority of our population. Those who had insufficient money for liquor, food, and household comforts, spent what they had on liquor. The misery of the meths drinkers, the drug addicts and the social misfits of today, even if added together, does not compare with the degradation caused by the excessive drinking in the last century.

In those days, generally speaking, those who were in a position to help did not feel they had any duty to involve themselves with the lower classes, who squandered what little they had on various forms of dissipation—a particularly hypocritical position when the debaucheries of high society, the drunken lord, the three bottle man, were still to be found in the haunts of the mighty. The newspapers did not write with any dedicated fervour against drink addiction. In fact, until comparatively recently, one had a column in which drunkenness was made a humorous daily feature. Here are two examples, not hilariously funny, but such copy must have helped the paper to sell.

Judge, Did you borrow £5 from this woman?
Man, No sir, I only asked for it so I could spend it on gin for her.
Magistrate, You hit your wife over the head with a bottle of beer.
Man in dock, No, not a bottle of beer, I'd drunk my half.'

The red-nosed staggerer was a comic character on the music-hall, the so-called funny post-cards and the cartoons.

Gin and porter were the staple diet of the time; even babies were given gin to keep them quiet, while porter was essential for health as Mr. Barrett told Elizabeth daily. Alcohol was a panacea for everything. Dickens, who had such a sympathy for the poor

Chapter III

made Sarah Gamp, not the depraved drunken character that she really was, but an amusing old woman ever demanding gin for the sake of her health and strength.

It is difficult to be too censorious of this form of indulgence when one realises the misery which constituted the normal life of the poor in towns where women and children suffered most from lack of money. In London, however, in 1898 there were two hundred more habitual women drunkards than men but, fortunately, this was not the pattern throughout the country. The very high death rate of young women at that time was attributed to tuberculosis, but now it is thought that many of those believed to have died from consumption may have been suffering from malnutrition. In the industrial areas and in the ports public houses sprang up with great rapidity to meet the incessant demand for drink. It seemed impossible that they could all pay; unfortunately they did! They were warm, fuggy, sawdusty and beery: above all they were welcoming. If there was no other friendly place to go, then naturally the family would flock there, for children were allowed in at any time until 1909 when the age of admittance to a licensed premises was stated to be fourteen. How much good this Act did is questionable, for after it had been passed the children were left outside to shelter in doorways or play to all hours in the streets.

The pubs opened before six a.m. to catch the men going to work; so it was beer for breakfast. They remained open until the small hours of the morning, or while there was anyone sufficiently sober to pay for the drinks. Even in the First World War they stayed open for 17½ hours per day. These places were second home to many, the men often put their feet up on the wooden seats, slept off their drunkenness and then were ready for work the next morning; others would stumble home just to sleep after having taken a big slice out of the wage packet.

It is difficult to know where the circle began: did they hasten to the grog-shop to escape the dreadful conditions of their homes, or were these hovel-like because of all the money given to the brewers? The most profitable business next to that of the publican was the pawnbroker: at the end of the row of public houses there would be 'Uncle', ready and waiting. By Wednesday the weekly wage was gone, and so began the great trek to the three golden balls—anything and everything was 'popped'. Children used to push hand carts stacked with goods, from boots to bedding, to be pawned. Redemption day was pay day, but the rate of interest charged was high as there was then no control of this. Week after week there were things that could not be reclaimed, the family's possessions became fewer and fewer, and the standard of living got lower and lower.

During her early social work Miss Weston had been aware of the harmfulness of alcohol, but as drunkenness was not rife in Bath she had not considered the question very deeply until she was asked by Miss Williams, a life-long friend, to speak on the importance of temperance. Miss Williams ran a mission in Avon Street, then one of the roughest parts of Bath, and at the hall would collect the outcasts of society—the gypsies, tramps and down-and-outs of the district. The audience was tough as Agnes realised when she spoke with feeling on the evils of intemperance. She was gratified at the end of her speech when so many came forward to sign the pledge. Among these was a chimney sweep, who swayed slightly, but was encouraged by his friends, one on either side, to sign. The sweep lifted up the pen, hesitated, then looked Agnes straight in the eyes and said, 'Have you signed this book?' Such a direct question took Miss Weston off her guard, 'Well, no, I sometimes have a glass of wine, but ... ' The damage had been done. 'Then if you haven't signed neither will I', and he staggered off probably to tell the story a dozen times over his beer. But there is an interesting sequel to this incident: many years later a lecturer was telling this story to an assembly, and giving it a sad end, for all thought that the chimney sweep would have drunk himself to death. Then a member of the audience stood up, and said 'I am that man, and you can give Miss Weston a message from me. The night that I walked out from her meeting was a turning point for me. I began to think about the stupid life I was leading, and so I gave up strong drink, and have never been tempted since'. It is worthy of record that the influence of this event was complementary, for that night long before when Frank Stephens, the chimney sweep, had left the hall in disgust, Agnes realised that she could not tell other people what to do if she were not prepared to do the same thing herself. She therefore signed the pledge, and shortly afterwards her sister Emily followed her example; their mother did not become a total abstainer until she was over 70, many years after both her daughters had pledged themselves.

Some months after her talk at Avon Street Agnes was at Devonport when the National Temperance League held an inaugural service to try to rouse enthusiasm for this cause among the men. Actually this good work had been started by the men themselves some years previously on board H.M.S. *Reindeer*. The Devonport meeting was held on 28 April 1873. The Lord Bishop presided over it, and among the celebrated assembly was Admiral Sir William King-Hall, a teetotaller of long standing.

There is much argument and confusion over the origin of the word 'teetotaller'. Richard Turny, a plasterer's labourer at Preston, Lancashire, in the midst of a philippic against what he called half measures said, 'I'll have nowt to do with this moderation—botheration pledge I'll be a reet down te-tee-total for ever'. 'Well done, Dick', said the Chairman, 'that shall be the name of our new pledge'. Another legend goes that Mr. Swindehurst of Preston—with an impediment in his speech—pronounced the word 't- t- total—which was adopted as a shibboleth.

Miss Weston promised to do all she could to help, and Mr. Sims, one of the League's organisers saw that she did it. He suggested that she should talk to the men on the decks of the ships—this was an unprecedented venture, a woman speaker on Her Majesty's ships? Regulations laid down that at any gathering the visiting speaker should be accompanied by the captain or the chaplain in case any mutinous or inflammatory words should be spoken. Then the speaker, if not exactly thrown overboard, could at least be hustled quickly away, but if a woman were speaking how could one handle her if the speech were not approved of? This was before the time of the militant suffragettes, when normal courtesies to the weaker sex were to be forgotten. Agnes promised that if permission were granted she would speak to the lads just as if she were their mother, but even this did not satisfy the Admiral, so he compromised. He said that she could hold a lunch time meeting in the Devonport Dockyard and talk to a group of men. If she could interest them, not lose her dignity, and say nothing that the captains of Her Majesty's ships could take exception to then she could talk to the ratings. Agnes agreed and held her meeting. Certainly she held the interest of her listeners, for at the conclusion of the short talk they asked her to speak to them again, and the chaplain, who was listening, reported that he was certain she would be a great success as a speaker on the decks. Permission was then granted. The Admiral undertook personally to vouch for Miss Weston's good conduct. We wonder what effect the chaplains of that era had on the men when it was considered that a strong, and therefore sober, Navy was a national insurance, but it seemed that for years no progress had been made towards this. A social worker of that time wrote that in his experience a few chaplains deserved the highest praise for the work they did amongst the lower deck and their influence, especially over the young lads with whom they came into contact, was far-reaching. The majority of the chaplains, unhappily, were completely out of touch with the men as they were more concerned with the pleasure of being naval officers and had no sense of vocation. The same writer recalled that when one chaplain found himself having tea with some men from his own ship after a meeting he was so embarrassed that neither he nor the men could communicate with one another. It is easy to see that in such circumstances no padre could truly lead his flock.

Agnes Weston never had this kind of difficulty; there was no barrier between her and the men because she cared for them and believed implicitly in her teachings. Her first visit was to H.M.S. *Impregnable* where she was greeted by Captain Wilson V.C. and his officers. The boys to whom she was to speak were sitting on the quarter deck, while she went up to the poop deck with the Captain. As she looked down on the lads, she was only aware of a sea of eager faces. On their part they saw a woman full of warmth and humanity whom they felt had their welfare at heart. This was the first time she had spoken afloat; everything was strange and she wrote in her diary that if ever she needed guidance it was then. As Agnes talked she knew she was being listened to by a sympathetic crowd and the only sound, apart from her own voice, was the screech of the gulls as they circled and swooped around the ship. At the end of her talk 250 lads came forward to sign the pledge. It was an experience that she never forgot. That this first visit was a success was fortunate, for otherwise subsequent talks might have been cancelled. Mr. Sims, never a laggard in his good works, went ahead with the planning of further talks and during 1873 she paid 38 visits to ships and government establishments. She triumphantly sent back to headquarters 1,600 pledges. With this, as with all she did, she started in a small way, but in no time at all the work had grown to enormous proportions. One very eventful meeting was called at Portsmouth by her very first blue-jacket pen friend, George Brown of H.M.S. *Crocodile,* to enable Agnes to meet many of the men with whom she had corresponded for years. George Brown's real name was George Dowkonott, for he was a Pole by birth and had adopted the name of a boatswain friend when he joined the British Navy. He had a most interesting life, for while he was in the Navy, he not only cared for the sick, as was his duty as a sick-berth attendant, but his work was far wider reaching. When in harbour, he would visit men who had had to leave the Navy because of illness and see parents who were eager to hear news of their lads; in fact he performed the duties of the modern welfare officer. When George Brown's years of service in the Royal Navy were ended he went as an assistant in the Liverpool Medical Mission where he continued his good work. His abilities there were so outstanding that a philanthropic business man, interested in the Mission, felt George Brown's skills could be better used if he had medical training and paid for him to go to America to train as a doctor. Brown received his medical degree and went back to Liverpool to continue work in the Medical Mission. In one of his letters to Agnes Weston he says, 'Isn't it wonderful that I, who for years was a blue-jacket, can now put M.D. after my name?'. But all that happened many years after their first encounter in Portsmouth where the hall was crowded with men whom Agnes was meeting for the first time. What they had expected to see she did not know, certainly someone older, for she had shown the understanding and tolerance in her letters of a far more mature woman. They greeted her with a rousing cheer and, after her speech and the signing of the pledges, one after another came to make themselves known to her and to tell her what her letters meant to them. That evening she made lifelong friends many of whom were to help her actively in her future work.

During the following year she visited H.M.S. *Topaze,* and when she had finished her talk the men, inspired by her words, hastened forward to sign the pledge. The Captain sent for a table on which to rest the book, but Agnes, eager to get the signatures just in case any should change their minds, used what she thought was the bread-tub and found out later that in mistake she had used the grog-tub. Sixty men signed; then a young lad came along, added his name, and patting the grog-tub on the side said, 'Here's another nail in your coffin'.

Agnes was a good sailor and when she was invited to speak she had to go and rough seas or heavy weather could be no excuse. On one occasion, when she was being rowed out to H.M.S. *Thalia,* she nearly came to her end through the fault of a cocksure midshipman; fortunately for her and the rest of the crew the officer of the watch saw the small boat's plight and sent out a steam launch to tow it in. After her meeting she was sent safely back in the steam launch, while the midshipman, very much in disgrace, remained on board. Years afterwards, when someone asked whether she was never overawed by gold-braided admirals, she replied, 'I really can't take them too seriously, you see I knew them nearly all when they were midshipmen, and somehow I can never imagine that they have grown up'.

It was while she was working for the National Temperance League among the ships and the government shore bases that Agnes heard of her father's death. She had just gone from Chatham to Portsmouth to visit Haslar Hospital when she received the telegram from her brother. One thing which helped to assuage her loss was the fact that her father died while he was still active in mind and body, for she knew how he would have hated to have been an invalid. Only a short time before his death he had begun to learn German and had enjoyed what he called this 'new adventure'.

In 1873 when Agnes began her work with the naval branches of the Temperance League, they could be counted on one hand but by 1877 the number had risen to 135 of which 112 were on the ships. By the end of the century there was a branch on every ship in the fleet and so her work in this field was fulfilled.

She was much praised by the Admiralty for her good work, but did not always get full co-operation from them. Some of the men had told her that given an adequate allowance in the place of the rum they would willingly forgo it, but the allowance had to be adequate. The sailors rejected the initial meagre offer of 1¼d. in lieu of two days' spirit. Agnes Weston pressed for 2d. a day recompense; this was rejected. It was not until July 1919, nine months after her death, that the men were offered not 2d. but 3d. a day as an alternative to the tot. She would have been delighted to have read the announcement which was received with great enthusiasm in the Navy. The day after the offer was made 146 men in the Signal School alone gave up the grog and accepted the payment.

As more Temperance branches, each with a local secretary, were established Agnes Weston's work in this sphere lessened, but she never gave up the fight to make the Navy sober. She made less personal visits to the men but reached a far greater number through her writings; every month a full page of *Ashore and Afloat,* her naval journal, was devoted to temperance news. She tried to interest her readers in this subject, either by informative passages, or by graphic stories of the importance of sobriety. Some of these were of a humorous nature, for she often said there was nothing Jack enjoyed more than a good joke.

To quote some random examples from her writings:

'Do you realise that the estimates last year [1908] for the great navies of the world, Great Britain, France, Germany, Italy, United States and Japan were £120,780,435, whereas Great Britain alone spent £160,000,000 on liquor!'

'Where there's drink there's danger', she headed one page in 1910 — a sentiment that is echoed today in the campaign against drunken driving.

'Is Britain spending sufficient on food [1911]?

Bread	£78,000,000
Butter and Cheese	£39,000,000
Milk	£34,000,000
Eggs	£11,000,000
Fruit	£10,000,000
A total of	£172,000,000
Alcoholic Liquor accounted for	£175,000,000

'Drunkenness is AN EXPENSIVE HABIT ...... a man who got drunk and violent made out to his sorrow the following account:

Doctor's bill for curing my wife and mending her ribs	£6.13s. 6d.
To buy extra things during wife's illness	£2. 8s. 0d.
To have smashed banister and door mended, and to pay damages to the landlord	£1.10s. 0d.
Pay a woman to look after wife and child	£1. 5s. 0d.
Loss of week's work	£1.10s. 0d.
For crockery broken	10s. 0d.
Fine plus costs	18s. 0d.
	£14.16s. 6d.

'On the other hand, see what you could do with the money spent on beer. If for one year a man who spent 3d. a day saved this, and bought a Christmas hamper to take home for the family, this is what he could buy with his savings ....

1 turkey, 8lb. beef, 1 ham, 4lb. sausages, 1 large Christmas pudding, 2 bushels of potatoes, 4 bottles of pickles, 4 jars of jam, 12lb. of sugar, 5lb. biscuits, 2 lb. coffee, 2lb. tea, 5lb. currants, 6lb. of sweets, 2 boxes of preserves, 1 parcel of pepper and spices, 100 oranges, 12lb. cheese, 12lb. rice, and in addition some fire wood, cwt. coal, matches and candles, some note paper and envelopes. Quite an impressive present to please the family with at Christmas!'

She was always eager to pass on cheerful news and in capital letters stated that the total number of indictable cases of drunkenness dropped from 12,747 in 1909 to 10,355 in 1910.

She read with pleasure, and published the praise given by a *Times* correspondent of the sailors from a cruiser when it visited Lisbon. He wrote of the quiet dignified behaviour of the men while on shore which excited universal admiration. An English observer in Lisbon also added his tribute, 'I must write to say I never saw a crew behave as well. They were perfect gentlemen and were a credit to their officers and country'.

Agnes ran what became almost a serial on the adventures of Mr. Arabi the much battered tea-pot used by a small party of teetotallers in the Egyptian war. It went with the men throughout the campaign, and during all that time they suffered no sickness because the boiling killed the germs in the tainted water and no amount of alcohol has such sterilizing effect. When the men of the

Chapter III

Naval Brigade returned on the *Inconstant* they brought the tea-pot home with them and when Agnes visited the ship it was proudly displayed on the mess-table.

But it was not until the First World War that the full results of her forty years' work were made evident. By that time 50,000 blue-jackets belonged to the Royal Naval Temperance Society and these were, as Agnes Weston said, 'Harbour lights to lesser craft uncertain of the way'.

IV

DURING HER Royal Naval Temperance Society meetings Agnes Weston met hundreds of blue-jackets. Most of the ships' companies were very responsive to her appeal, but of all the ships she visited, none gave her a more hearty welcome than the men of the H.M.S. *Dryad*. On this gunboat she found many dedicated Christians who had a marked influence on the rest of the crew. Agnes was not, therefore, in the least surprised when she received a request to meet a deputation from that ship. She really gave it little thought, imagining that they wanted to plan fresh meetings to boost their temperance campaign. She invited them to Stoke and entertained them in Mrs. Wintz's drawing room which, by that time, was becoming as important, in its way, as the Naval Board room. When Agnes heard what the men wanted she was flabbergasted. A Petty Officer had been chosen as spokesman and he carefully expounded their plan. The men wanted her to open a rest house for the sailors. They told her it ought to be near the Dockyard and a teetotal establishment. When she did not respond at once, the spokesman continued to point out the good effect such a place would have on the young sailors; they knew that she was interested in the lower decks' welfare and the only person they could approach: — Please, what did she say? She was conscious that by not instantly agreeing to their plans with enthusiasm she was disappointing them, but she wondered if they realised what they were asking her to do. The more she thought about it the greater the difficulties appeared. For one thing she would have to devote her entire life to the work and she was not sure if she wanted to do this. She knew that if she undertook the task she would never again have any private life but only such moments as could be snatched from the rush of work. Then there was the question of capital—such a proposition would be costly. Supposing, too, that she started it and the scheme failed, then she would have lost everything and especially any good influence she had over the young sailors. Nothing spreads faster than the news of failure. There would be opposition from many quarters to such a home and she wanted to be certain that she could combat the fiercest criticism. In later years she did, in fact, receive some harsh censure but she was then immune to it and much too busy to listen to such calumny and brushed it aside as of no consequence.

With all these thoughts rushing through her mind she knew that she must temporise. 'Give me a week to think it over', she said, 'and by then I shall be able to give you an answer.' With this the men reluctantly had to be content.

Agnes Weston discussed the startling suggestion with Sophia Wintz, and after much earnest thought and prayer, and the promise of Sophia's help, decided to try to do what the men of the *Dryad* wished. When the sailors returned after the week, Agnes told them she would do her very best to fulfil their request. They were not surprised; they had been certain of the answer.

Having made up her mind, she had no more doubts; it was to be the most exciting venture of her life. She began to look for suitable premises, large and cheap, near the Dockyard. There was no choice because there was only one vacant building anywhere near the Dockyard Gates, an empty dilapidated shop that had once been a Co-op. grocery store. It looked anything but inviting, and was flanked by public houses. Opposite too was a row of pubs and the ever-present pawn-shop! Besides the shop there were some large sheds at the back, and across a small courtyard two very tiny cottages. It was this or nothing, and the owners knew its worth. They offered the premises on lease for one year, with the option to buy at the end of that period. Agnes agreed. She paid the first year's rent out of her private income.

She was determined to try to make up for some of the hardships the sailors had to bear, the wet, the cold, the crowded living quarters, the inadequate badly cooked rations. Her Rest House would be warm, bright, gay, comfortable and clean; the food would be well cooked and appetisingly served. Once while inspecting the shop with Canon Head, a great friend, she was telling him how one day the games room and a library would be there, while the cabins would go tier upon tier. As there was so much that was wanted, she was not sure how it could all be fitted in. He stopped her, and asked, 'Shall we just ask God about it?' They knelt in the musty old shop, and prayed for God's help.

She knew that visions do not become actualities without a good deal of work, worry and money. Of the first she was never afraid, of the second she once told a helper that troubles and mistakes begat experience which is a priceless possession that no man can take away. She appealed for funds through the temperance magazines and also in *The Christian*. The editor of this paper, R.C. Morgan, was sympathetic to the cause and gave the appeal much publicity. A friend of his promised to cap every hundred pounds contributed with a five pound note. The money began to trickle in and directly there was sufficient the House was started. At first Agnes lived at the Wintz's home, and she and Sophia went daily to supervise the work, but as more funds were needed Agnes travelled the length and breadth of Britain talking to people who might help. Eventually the £6,000 needed was collected, the shop bought, and to use her own words, 'the old place completely transmogrified'.

Agnes Weston has been described as one of the greatest philanthropic workers of all times; she not only collected large funds from the public but ploughed her own money into helping the sailors. The yield was great for she lived to see the blue-jacket become one of the most respected members of society.

She spent little money on herself and I have a letter from one of her cousins which says: 'I stayed at a very modest hotel in Scotland, and in the visitors' book there is an entry to show that cousin Agnes had stayed there while seeking funds for her work. I am pleased that she sought such inexpensive accommodation'. Agnes found the Scots very ready to help: towards the Devonport House they subscribed over £1,000.

Sophia Wintz was invaluable helping with the accounts, for she was a good business woman. She also had great gifts for planning, organising and fitting up the rooms, and at first made herself responsible for all the administration until a young accountant,

Chapter IV

Arthur Wren, offered to help with the financial affairs and gradually took over the whole of the book-keeping; this he continued to do for the next forty years.

Subscription lists and balance sheets were audited by professional accountants, and were published annually, for Agnes Weston was always acutely aware that she was only the custodian of all money collected for the benefit of the blue-jackets. She and Sophia paid for their keep, gave generously from their own purses, and worked voluntarily—it is difficult, therefore, to think that anyone could have thought that they were lining their own pockets, as was suggested by disgruntled publicans in Devonport. By 1876 no one would have recognised the old grocery shop. It had been changed into a very attractive hostel. In the restaurant there were gay curtains, marble topped tables which shone invitingly, and settles, very popular at that time. Mirrors and gilt decorations added brightness and gaiety to the room.

The kitchen was upstairs, and so speaking tubes were installed and service lifts fitted to ensure that the food would be hot when it reached the tables. So much of the success of the House would depend on the standard of the cuisine, and Miss Weston was fortunate in having the help of the School of Cookery at South Kensington, who sent members to Devonport to help train the cooks.

On the first floor there was a large smoking, games, reading and writing room. Agnes looked forward to the time when there would be a suite of such rooms but in the meantime one would have to suffice. The cottages were turned into sleeping quarters and, inadequate though this might be, it was a start.

Many asked Agnes Weston who was going to be asked to open the House, but she said, 'No formal opening, let's wait a year and see how things shape before we have a flourish of trumpets.' On 7 May, a thanksgiving service was held in the small hall, and afterwards three blue-jackets asked Agnes if they could be the first ones to sleep at the House. She demurred as the place was not actually open, but when the men pointed out that they had received special leave from their Captain, they said surely she could throw red tape overboard for once. She did, she threw it overboard, and it sank, and for the rest of her life's work it was never seen again. Later the three sailors gave her a photograph signed, 'The first birds to roost at the Sailors' Rest'. She hung the picture and agreed that it was a good name ...... 'The Sailors' Rest'.

On Monday, 8 May, the doors were open at 5 a.m. and in crowded the men to be met with a mixture of delicious smells of hot freshly baked bread, coffee, sizzling bacon, eggs and sausages, as well as a variety of cold food from meat dishes to sandwiches. Sophia Wintz, in her description of the opening, wrote that you could have walked on the heads of the men on that first morning, and that, although the popularity of the Rest was maintained, never again was there quite such a crush. Agnes Weston was determined, from the start, that the Sailors' Rest should pay its way; this was to be no charitable institution as she was sure the sailors did not wish it. Food and beverages were to be paid for in the restaurant which was to be open to anyone. In the first year the total takings amounted to £1,998. The recreation rooms, on the other hand, were for sailors only and writing paper, envelopes, reading matter and games were provided free. There was no membership fee: this was not a club, it was a Home, in the proper sense of the word, for sailors from any country.

The Rest consisted of the Hall and the Institute, which were closely linked. The Hall was used for Bible classes, services, temperance gatherings and social meetings, to which the sailors were urged to take their wives and children. The Institute consisted of the restaurant, the recreation rooms and the cabins. These with their clean beds, chairs, pictures, texts, and bright strips of mats were much appreciated. Agnes said, 'It is privacy that they want,' and one stalwart man-o'-war said to her, 'Miss Weston, when I got into my cabin and locked the door I knew that I'd got it to myself, no boatswain's mate could pipe me away to duty, I felt as happy as if I were in heaven'.

The opening of the first Rest was anything but easy. Sophia Wintz, who had done so much of the organising said, 'Woe to the simple heart who, starting a Home or an Institution, imagines that with getting the building and fitting it up the worst troubles are over. Generally the difficulties only then commence'. But gradually with patience and commonsense the difficulties were overcome. For instance Agnes wanted ex-naval men and sailors' widows to work as staff. They were not trained personnel, but she thought they would understand the ways of the naval man better than a civilian domestic staff however highly trained. Sophia found the initial period very hard but later admitted that Agnes' decision was right.

Agnes Weston's staff remained with her for years, and she says truly that they formed a force to help towards the comfort of the men. She encouraged the staff to know the men by name; to try to know them personally so that when they returned after a period they would not feel forgotten. One old sailor, in a letter to the author, tells how he went back to the Devonport Rest after an absence of several years and was welcomed by the receptionist at the desk with a cheery smile, and 'Nice to see you back, Mr. Wade. Now, let me see, it's a back cabin you like, quieter—much quieter', Mr. Wade felt that he was really home again.

Agnes thought of every possible way to make the place welcoming and among the little aids to homeliness she counted a parrot and a retriever dog. Polly called to everyone, 'Walk in Jack; glad to see you; have a cup of coffee', whether the caller was a sailor or a Prince as was the case when Prince Edward and Prince George, as cadets, paid an informal visit to the Devonport Rest. The Royal visitors were much amused by the parrot, took her advice and had coffee and large helpings of plum-duff. It was some years later when Agnes Weston was visiting Trinity College, Cambridge, that the Prince of Wales asked her to go to his room where he then enquired about her work and laughingly asked whether the plum-duff was as good as it had been when he was a cadet on the *Britannia*.

But poor Polly was killed by kindness, she would eat anything, and the more she ate the more she was given. Ham and sausages—hardly the diet for a parrot—were her favourite food. Hector, the retriever, used to meet the men at the door wagging his welcome; he seemed most friendly except to the dog owned by the Commander of the *Cambridge*. This was his arch-enemy, and Hector, a fine swimmer, would jump off the bridge at Stonehouse Creek and swim across the harbour to the *Cambridge* for the sole purpose of fighting the Commander's dog. Much to the pleasure of the sailors Hector was invariably the winner. But poor Hector like Polly was killed by kindness, he loved jam tarts and would beg for them as long as anyone would feed him: he just overate and died.

After the opening, Agnes took all matters of policy upon herself with the help and advice of Sophia Wintz, and it was not until many years later that a Board of Trustees was formed to formulate future policy and maintain present administration. During the formative years Agnes, although open to suggestion and ready to take sound advice, considered it her duty to be responsible for the decisions which she believed would help the majority. She was never a committee woman, and used to say that Noah would never have finished the Ark if he had had a committee.

Many people advised her that she should not allow drunks into the building but she said there was a place for them; they were someone's boys and any good the Rest could do them it should. Agnes Weston maintained that the blue-jacket must feel free to come and go as he pleased whether drunk or sober, and whatever his condition must be given the same kindly consideration by the staff. She did what she could to prevent drunkenness, but knew that condemnation would not help. Her hope was that kindness shown to a drunken man might make him think that people were really trying to help him.

'I'm sorry I was three sheets in the wind last night Miss Weston, but you see it was my birthday, and I celebrated with the lads.'

She smiled. 'You'll be an old man soon, for that is the third birthday you've had in two weeks!'

Drunks were picked up in the gutters and taken to the Rest where a shakedown was always found for them even if the beds were full. One night a man staggered in reeling under the weight of his load wrapped in oil-skin. 'Whatever have you got there?' Miss Weston asked. 'It's me mate, I picked him up in Plymouth the worse for drink and as we didn't have the price of a cab, I've carried him here. The police stopped me on the way: "What you got there, Government property?" "Not unless you call him Government property," and I leant me pal up against the wall and showed his face. "Where you taking him?" they asked; when I said, "To Mother Weston's," all was well. But what a weight!'

Agnes was much touched by this man's action and wrote in her *Life among the Blue-jackets,* 'What an act of practical Christianity that was on the part of that man, and I only hope that in our way we can live up to it'.

When she was returning to the Rest one night the only other occupant of the tramcar was a huge blue-jacket, sprawled across the seats. He was 'Fighting Charlie', renowned throughout Devonport for his heavy drinking and his quick 'right'. The conductor looked at Charlie, but had no intention of asking for his fare. 'What will you do with him?' Miss Weston asked. 'Oh the driver and I'll try to get him in the gutter at the end of the journey, and the patrol will pick him up.' 'Come on Charlie,' she said at the Rest stop, and had the forethought to move away quickly. She had been right, Charlie's fists were doubled in a second. 'Now come on Charlie, it's only me', 'Why if it ain't me Mother Weston,' and carefully she helped him out of the tram. The weight was too much for her but a friendly sailor took Charlie's other arm and they got him into the Rest and off to bed. The next day, full of good intentions, Charlie told Agnes Weston he had turned over a new leaf; he was going to give up drinking; give up fighting; let her be his mother and father, and if he ever heard a man say one word against her he would knock him down, crush him, stamp on him, be he as big as a church.

Taking their lead from Miss Weston, the staff made every effort to keep the man who was a little drunk from going out and possibly getting in trouble with the Naval police. One night a half sober blue-jacket threw down half a crown on the counter and called for a glass of half and half, and to make it stiff and make it quick. The woman server said understandingly, 'We haven't the half and half you want, try some of ours'.

'What's that then?'

'Would you like a hot or cold drink?'

'You seem to have more than cold water, I'd like a jorum of something hot.'

'Would you like a cup of coffee?'

'Yes, it's a long time since I've had much in the coffee line.'

'Are you a Devonshire man?' she asked.

'Sure, I'm West country to the back-bone.'

'Then you'll like coffee with Devonshire cream.'

The man was completely won over, it was a long time since anyone had taken so much trouble over his wants, and when he was charged only a penny he could scarcely believe it. 'If Miss Weston goes on like this she'll soon be out of business', he said, but the server explained that half of the penny was profit. The man returned again and again with many of his mates and became a strong supporter of the Rest. He said that on his first visit he had received the only kind words he had heard for months.

The next thing that Agnes Weston had to decide was who should be admitted to the Hall, and her answer was simple: everyone was welcome, whatever his creed, or even if he had no creed at all. She knew, as she said 'Jack is a shy fellow, and would run if he thought he was going to be preached at', so emphasised that he must be free to come and go as he pleased. The work was carried out on a truly non-denominational basis; one night the platform would be occupied by a clergyman, on another by a lay preacher, sometimes by an Army or Naval officer or by a working man. Agnes summed it up by saying, 'Our work is a pioneer work; we often get them when they are far out of the way, and we present the simple truth of the Gospel in an unconventional manner'.

Work inside the Rest settled down to a happy routine, in fact it became known as the three C's, Comfort, Coffee and Company. The more popular the Rest became the more the neighbouring publicans tried to win back their lost trade; they gave away pints of beer; they put half crowns in some of the pots then filled the jars with ale so that some drinkers would get something for nothing. It became quite a battle, the beer jug *v.* the coffee pot, and the coffee pot won. Many said it was wicked to stop the poor men from having their beer, but years later when drunkenness was decreasing sailors were asked on several occasions if they would like a small quantity of beer on the premises, and the answer was always an emphatic NO. None answered this more decidedly than the non-abstaining seamen who frequented the Institute in large numbers; they argued that if alcohol were ever introduced the whole place would be spoilt.

When the publicans failed to close the Rest by forcing the customers away, they threatened to break all the windows, but Miss Weston did not argue or ask for police protection—she wisely increased the insurance.

The Rest had not been opened long when it became obvious that more sleeping quarters were necessary. Having no debts, and with the building fund looking healthy, Agnes set about having a tall block of dormitories built in the courtyard behind the Hall; months later a cottage was bought in Dockwall Street and altered to provide more sleeping accommodation.

Still the popularity of the Rest grew and bigger premises were urgently needed if no one was to be turned away. But it was difficult to spread; the public houses and the pawn shop opposite had disappeared because of the dropping-off of business; then it was thought that a big gin palace was going to be built. Whether this was rumour, or whether permission to build such a place was refused, is not clear, but opposite the Rest a tailor's shop and an ironmonger's shop were erected. The only possible way the Rest could spread was towards the Dockyard Gate, but three public houses would have to be removed. These were the *Napier's* Inn, the *Royal Navy Rendezvous,* and the *Dock Gates'* Inn. 'Do shake out a reef Miss Weston', pleaded the blue-jackets, 'we must have a bigger place; we often have to look out the softest plank to sleep on'. This was true, for practically every day all bed tickets were sold before noon. Agnes realised that if she tried to buy the three public houses she would have to purchase the licences as well. Then one morning, quite unexpectedly, she had a letter postmarked Fiume, from Robert Whitehead the inventor of the Whitehead torpedo, enclosing a cheque for £1,000. He wrote that he had heard of her effort to enlarge the Devonport Rest and hoped that his cheque would help to knock a hole in one of her stumbling blocks. This cheque was followed by another for £1,000 from the philanthropic Mrs. Langworthy of Manchester. These were supplemented by a stream of subscriptions ranging from a shilling sent by a mother whose son had found comfort at the Rest to large sums subscribed from ships all over the world.

There were packets of pennies from the sailor boys, a sovereign wrapped in silver paper from a bride-to-be who was sure her fiancé would never have been able to have saved for the home if Miss Weston had not taken care of his savings for him. In addition to these contributions Sophia Wintz went to many of the big cities to talk at meetings and drawing-room gatherings. Agnes marvelled at Sophia's fortitude, 'My friend looked so young and delicate,' she said, 'yet she had the pluck of the bravest man in the service.' Often she would travel at night, talk at one or two meetings during the day, and then be off again.

Eventually, with sufficient funds, Agnes Weston bid for the three houses and their licences. While she was waiting to see if her offer had been accepted she received a five pound note from the outfitter opposite. 'A lucky gift,' he said, and expressed the hope that she had secured the licences as he took a personal interest in the good being done for the naval men.

For £7,000 the houses were hers. The next step was their demolition, and ironically the rubble from them was used to fill up the government trenches in Plymouth into which many a drunk had fallen and broken his neck.

In 1888 the cornerstone was laid by Admiral H.G. Grant, C.B., and a magnificent building was erected. The frontage was indeed imposing, and over the main doorway was a turret on the spire of which was a weather vane in the shape of an old Viking warship. As well as a restaurant there was a coffee room, reading and writing rooms, a separate room for games, and a quiet corner for chess. The cabins were as spick and span as always and at 6*d.* a night they were always fully booked.

For the sailor boys in training there was a separate wing with its own entrance. Special visits were arranged for the lads on Thursdays and Sundays, and these gave unmitigated pleasure. Many old sailors in talks with the author have given vivid descriptions of their afternoons at Miss Weston's. The teas she provided for them remain as clear today as at the time they had them. In their own words, 'Such a blow-out you never saw, we ate till we were ready to burst!'. There were games, competitions and fun on the Thursdays, and on the Sundays a short service. Agnes was emphatic on the length of this, 'Make it not more than an hour, and you will have the boys' attention', she would say to her helpers. She wrote later that one of the most touching experiences of her life was to hear the beautiful clear voices of those sailor boys as they sang the hymns. One of those boys, now very much an 'old boy', said that what was so important to them was meeting people not attached to the training ship and feeling part of the outside world.

A visitor once said to her, 'Why it's boys, boys everywhere', and Agnes replied, 'That's just how I want it, a real home for them when they come ashore, and a place of safety which must rejoice their mothers' hearts'. Often there were two hundred boys sitting down to tea, the dining-room packed from stem to stern. The day the boys passed into men's service they had an extra special party laid on by the staff of the Rest, and, according to some, this made up for all the hardships of the years of training.

Just before the close of the century the Prince of Wales paid a formal visit to the Devonport Rest. He saw and admired everything that had been provided for the men, especially the cabins, and before he left he made the following entry in the visitors' book:

'I am much impressed by the admirable management and excellence of this institution. Albert Edward.'

By the turn of the 20th century the original Sailors' Rest was showing signs of collapse, and it was therefore pulled down. In its place was built a large Hall, to be known as the Queen Victoria Memorial Hall, and above it were tiers of cabins; this new building was joined to the main Rest. On 17 January 1905 the Hall was opened by Admiral Lord Charles Beresford. He was certainly the right person to ask to officiate, for his breezy, nonchalant manner appealed to the men; he was said to have been the most popular Admiral since Nelson.

Lord Beresford told his vast audience that the new block of Hall and cabins had cost £20,000, every penny of which had been collected by the voluntary work of Miss Weston and Miss Wintz, and went on to describe the mental and physical efforts needed to undertake such work. The Devonport Rest had cost in all £120,000, and was by far the largest Naval teetotal establishment in the world. He said that he could not tell people often enough that the Rest was entirely self-supporting, and that any profit made was equally shared between a building fund and a widows' and orphans' fund. He also said that the Admiralty was to begin two-year commissions and the men were to have increased leave so that families were not separated for such long periods. Lord Beresford knew this would meet with Miss Weston's approval. He concluded his speech by saying that Miss Weston and Miss Wintz had shown to all concerned just what the blue-jacket wanted, and he, Charles Beresford, was proud to be associated with the work.

A Hall to seat 600, sleeping accommodation for 800, and a most popular restaurant, all at the Devonport Rest, which according to W.S. Caine, M.P., the Civil Lord of the Admiralty, saved the country £1,000,000 a year and did good for the men that was above monetary calculation.

'All this', Agnes said, of the Devonport Rest, 'came from the blue-jackets' wish and the blue-jackets' prayers; is it any wonder that it has been dedicated to the Glory of God and the good of the Service'.

V

UNHAPPILY THE circumstances which led to the establishment of a Sailors' Rest in Portsmouth started with a national tragedy—the loss of the frigate *Eurydice* in 1878.

Agnes Weston never envisaged opening a Rest in Portsmouth when she met Mrs. Marcus Hare in Yorkshire in March 1878. She was in fact still recovering from the labours of opening the Devonport Rest and a branch house at Keyham and from travelling north to raise more funds for Naval welfare. She found much enthusiasm for this project, and people who attended her meetings were very willing to contribute to the needs of the sailors, realising that the safety of the nation depended on a sober and efficient Navy, which could only be achieved if some alternative forms of recreation and entertainment were provided for the sailors to combat the bad influences of the public houses in the home ports.

Mrs. Marcus Hare, one of Agnes Weston's main organisers for Naval welfare, was wife of the captain of the *Eurydice* a training frigate, at that time on her voyage home from the West Indies. The *Eurydice,* with her twenty-six guns, was a ship of which the nation had been very proud when launched in 1843. A poet wrote a paean of praise to her which ended with the lines:—

> Hail to thee, modern beauty hail,
> Success and honour with thee sail,
> Till as of old both land and sea,
> Ring with thy name—*Eurydice.*

Thirty-five years later her name did ring throughout the land, but not with the joy intoned by the poet, for while Mrs. Hare was hastening south to meet her husband at Portsmouth she learnt that the frigate had been sunk in a squall off the Isle of Wight. The news was worse than she might have anticipated, for out of a total crew of 320 only two had survived, neither of whom was her husband. Many months later when one of the survivors was describing the tragedy to Agnes Weston he told her how the Captain, after giving the order to abandon ship, had knelt in prayer as the ship went down. 'I'm not a religious man,' he said, 'but if ever there was a Christian then it was our Captain'.

On hearing the tragic news Agnes abandoned her meetings in the north and travelled south to see if there was anything she could do to alleviate the suffering of the bereaved. She had known many of the young men of the crew for she had visited the ship just before it had sailed for the West Indies; she had spoken on the need for temperance and helped to start the ship's branch of the Naval Temperance Society.

She visited the parents and dependents of the dead and gave what help and comfort she could. As she moved around the town she became acutely aware that there was work in abundance for her to do there. She went from one mean street to another, into one house of mourning after another, witnessing much sorrow, and words she had learned years before came back to her: 'When God has work to be done He trains the workers and sometimes the training may seem long, but He never makes a mistake and He clears the way day by day.' Perhaps those words were never more apt for her than at that moment.

It took five months for the frigate to be salvaged. The Admiral Superintendent of the Portsmouth Dockyard, Rear Admiral Francis John Foley, detailed Charles Beresford to undertake the task. In his *Memoirs,* he relates how honoured he felt to undertake this duty, for as a young cadet, he had learnt to heave a lead aboard the *Eurydice* when she had been moored off Haslar Creek, and he had been so happy training in her. Of course Beresford had never imagined that it would be his sad duty to salvage her wreck. He says that the newly invented wire hawsers were used in practice for the first time and they worked most efficiently. When the ship was finally beached the pledge cards and temperance books were discovered in reasonable condition, and were given to Agnes, but

Chapter V

they soon disintegrated on exposure, though not before she had been able to read the names of the dead. When the Captain's desk was prised open it was found that among other papers was a book in which he had composed some poems, the last started with the words 'There's sorrow, there's sorrow at sea ...'.

During her stay in Portsmouth Agnes Weston had been the welcome guest of Sarah Robinson who had turned a derelict inn into a comfortable home for soldiers during their off duty. The premises she had taken over was the once notorious *Fountain* Inn in the High Street. Agnes was naturally interested in Sarah's work because it was comparable to that she and Sophia were doing in Devonport, although on a very much smaller scale, and Agnes knew a great deal about the needs of the soldier from her sister Emily who was engaged in army welfare work in the West country. Sarah beseeched Agnes to start a Rest Home for sailors near the Portsmouth Dockyard; she needed little persuasion for the more she saw of the Portsea area the more urgently she knew she must act. Portsmouth, at that time, was divided into four distinct areas, a separation caused more by the occupation of the people than by any geographical division. Southsea, where the Wintz family had settled when they returned from Germany, has already been mentioned; Old Portsmouth, which was centred around the High Street, was commonly known as the 'Parade Ground' of the town, for it was the headquarters of the Army. Kingston and Landport was the shopping centre, where most of the Dockyard workers lived. The last section, and by far the smallest, was Portsea. It was there that Agnes's interest lay. It was known as the Lower Deck and was roughly triangular in shape. One side was Charlotte Street, usually called 'Bloody Row', because of the extraordinary number of butcher shops and the slaughter houses which backed them. It was a cheap-jack market during the day and a scene of great depravity at night. Drunken sailors would dance in the streets with girls, exchanging garments during their revels until, overcome by alcohol and excitement, all would fall in a helpless heap. The crowd would watch the bawdiness of the scene with avid interest until someone dragged the girls away, and the blue-jackets were taken, often frog-marched, to the naval cells. The crowd used to the scene, drifted away when the excitement was over. The base of the Portsea triangle was the Commercial Road and the third side

Queen Street. This street was named in honour of Queen Anne who, when visiting the town with her Consort, had given the shipwrights permission to build their houses, therefore countermanding a refusal by Governor Gibson who had threathened to turn the guns on them if they 'put brick upon brick', to quote his own words. It was said that although Queen Street was quiet in the day time, there were few worse streets in the whole world at night, nor few courts worse than those huddled around the street. 'They are', says one writer, 'diseased spots which fester and corrupt, where germs of every kind collect, and it is here that our sailors spend their time. These places of such ill repute flourish because of the number of unmarried men in the Navy especially prone to temptation because of the very manner of their lives and because nothing is offered to substitute for this so-called pleasure.' It was estimated that at the time this was written, there were ten thousand sailors in the port, and six thousand troops and marines in other parts of the town.

Charlotte Street and Queen Street both led to the Dockyard, which had been started in the 13th century by King John, who after peremptorily ordering that the docks of Portsmouth should be enclosed by a strong wall, soon lost interest in the project. Not until the reign of Henry VII, was commenced what was to become the modern dockyard of today.

Just outside the Main Gate was an area known as the 'Devil's Acre', because during the time of impressment it was often a scene of brutality and violence; later, when sailors came ashore from pay-off with their pockets full of money they were preyed upon by hordes of harpies who infested the place. Sarah Robinson thought that Devil's Acre was where Agnes should try to start a home, but the latter preferred to look for some sort of accommodation in the Commercial Road where crowds of sailors congregated.

There were throngs of them, many just walking aimlessly up and down, having nowhere to go, possibly because they were so short of money. It was certainly the busiest street in the South outside London and was known as the Regent Street for the Navy. Day and night it was full of bustle—it was without doubt the pulse of the port, albeit a feverish one. The bigger shops were open until midnight—the smaller ones all night. There were theatres and

Chapter V

music-halls, peep-shows, flea circuses, exhibitions of the fattest woman in the world, the smallest, the hairiest, the boy with two heads, the boy with three legs—in fact all the excitement and grotesqueness of life was in the Portsmouth Commercial Road. 'Everything here', thought Agnes, 'that is—except a vacant building'. Anxiously she scanned the property in the lower part of the road, but it never came on the market and an auctioneer whom she consulted told her 'it is so valuable it passes from father to son, from hand to hand you might say'.

She was not put off by this warning, but continued to ask and to look. Then she heard that a very old building, once a music hall, was to be let. Nowhere could have looked more unpromising, but to Agnes at that time anything would do and she rented it without hesitation. She knew from experience that the most unlikely place can be made inviting by work and organisation. But even she was a little dismayed when she had taken the premises and walked round to see what had to be done: the old Co-op. shop in Devonport had been a palace by comparison. The hall had a stage and proscenium arch both in the last stage of decay; there were holes in the floor through which came the stench of sewer gas; an army of rats had taken charge of the entire building.

Sophia Wintz came from Devonport with some of the workers from the Rest; members of the Naval Temperance League, who heard what was to be done, volunteered to help. Soon the place began to look habitable. Floor boards were fixed, a war waged on the rats, chairs mended, walls scrubbed and painted. New tables were bought and a counter installed for the coffee urns and tea pots. There it was then ready for the men, certainly not elaborate, but the ratings were delighted to have it, inadequate though it was. They swarmed in until there was barely breathing space. Refreshments were cheap, the place bright, warm and welcoming. As there was a stage Miss Weston thought concerts would be a good way of keeping the blue-jackets happy. Two or three nights a week there was entertainment all contributed by the sailors themselves: songs, recitations, juggling acts and acrobatic turns. The men loved it, but Miss Weston went, as she said, through a good deal of fire for people criticised her and said she was wrong—wicked almost—to encourage such forms of jollity. The more she thought about it the more she was convinced that she was right, so she announced that the concerts would proceed as usual and she would preside over them. Seldom did the men let her down and then, she would say fondly, only because of their high spirits.

The place was busy during the day and crowded out at night; there was no doubt about its popularity, but Agnes was concerned because there were no sleeping quarters and no room to build any. When the men left to return to their ships they had to walk along streets where pimps and prostitutes abounded. Agnes Weston was a realist and much as she liked and admired the young sailor she had no illusions about him. She knew that if clean comfortable cabins were to be had on the premises, he would turn in there for the night after a big hot supper, followed by an enjoyable concert. If he had to go out in the cold and walk a mile or so to his ship, he might well wake up in the morning in some insalubrious brothel, minus his wallet. But for the time being there was nothing she could do about it.

Eventually a carpenter who was doing some alterations at the little Rest, told Miss Weston of a man who was very interested in the work of the two ladies and would be willing to sell a building in the very heart of Commercial Road and would like to speak privately to her as soon as possible. Hurriedly Miss Weston went to see him. He received her very courteously and said that he had watched with amazement the way that she and her friend had carried on their work, and what they were doing could only be for the good of the men and ultimately for the good of the country. He went on to say that he would like to further the work by offering her a building he had for sale at a reasonable price. She accepted with alacrity. The deal was soon closed. The only thing lacking was the capital. It was difficult to realise where it was coming from. Then Agnes remembered Mr. Müller of Bristol and how his faith fed the orphans in his care, for when there was no breakfast they would pray and never once was their prayer unanswered, for even before the prayers were finished there would be a farmer at the door with a supply of grain and vegetables. She knew that like Müller she had faith, and by the first post on the day after the premises were bought, Agnes was invited to talk at the drawing-room meeting at the home of Anthony Denny. His lovely reception room in his house in Connaught Place, London, was crowded. Before the meeting Mr. Denny had asked Miss

Chapter V

Weston what she needed to start this new residential Rest in Portsmouth; at the end of the meeting he handed her a cheque for £1,050, fifty pounds more than the sum she had named! She was very grateful to the donors and little overwhelmed by their generosity. At first she felt somewhat guilty at having collected such a large sum until she remembered that one of the audience had spent twenty times as much on one racehorse the previous week.

The foundation of the Portsmouth Rest was laid and the building went ahead. To raise the enormous amount of money needed to complete this work Agnes and Sophia travelled week after week talking to various gatherings, explaining what was to be done for the sailors and asking for funds. While one of the friends would be doing this very difficult job the other would be mothering at Devonport or supervising the work at Portsmouth.

On 13 June 1881, the Portsmouth Rest was ready to be opened. The men were well pleased with it; they said that they were commissioning the ship, and that once finished they would see that it was kept afloat. They wanted to open the Rest themselves and could not see why a person of rank should be asked to perform the ceremony, when he or she could not be nearly as interested in the building as the blue-jackets themselves. Logical as always, Agnes said, 'Well it was designed for the lads, they shall open it themselves.' So the inauguration was a nautical and enthusiastic ceremony. Sailors swarmed in: the big room was filled to overflowing, they sat on the windowsills, on the banisters and stood on the stairs. Their cheers rang out when a representative from H.M.S. *Excellent* said, "We've no pennant, but we can fancy it's hoisted. Now then, mates, cheer the pennant and the new ship—and however far we shall go we shall find her here when we get back again. We'll rally round the place, and help Miss Weston and Miss Wintz to carry on the work: it shall be a long pull, and a strong pull and a pull altogether'.

The Sailors' Rest had been so urgently needed that it was immediately accepted and became a Portsmouth landmark. On the very top burnt a red light, a beacon to call the lads home, and Agnes Weston used it so, for she'd say, 'Now get back tonight, follow the red light then you'll know the way, and if you see two red lights then try to get here as hard as you can, for you'll need a shake down then alright'.

Her Portsmouth workers have told me that often if she heard of a young lad the worse for drink who was likely to be picked up by the patrols, she would put on her bonnet and cape and set off to take him back to the Rest. Invariably she returned with two, one on each arm, and it was remarkable how she was able to manage them, for although a strong woman, she was not tall, and often these young blue-jackets would be towering above her as she herded them along. Safely inside the Rest she would see the drunks were looked after for, as she said, they were some mother's sons.

Agnes Weston was most unpopular with the Queen Street prostitutes; they would throw mud or stones at her as she walked up from the Dockyard, but she took no notice and gradually the animosity died down, or perhaps it was that the district improved. The Portsmouth police, on the other hand, worked well with her right from the start. They would bring along as many drunks as they could, and often would call out to the night watchman, 'Careful how you open the door we've another dozen waiting here!' But good was being done, and people, especially those living in the ports and those in authority, were becoming aware that the old tough sailor was giving way to the newer and more civilised one.

Although the Rest was so successful it was obviously not large enough; a big hall was needed for meetings and concerts but until the money was found it could not be built. In the meantime Miss Weston put a large marquee in the courtyard behind the main building which had to suffice until, years later, a magnificent hall was built.

The Rest eventually grew to become a huge block of buildings, but during its development top priority was for sleeping accommodation, so as funds became available extra cabins were added. A fine new block was subscribed for and built to commemorate the Queen's Diamond Jubilee. But no matter how much accommodation was added there was never sufficient, and the blue-jackets in Portsmouth, as in Devonport, would go to Agnes and say, 'Mother, surely you can add a bit more to the Rest, we can't sleep more than six on a table, and then we can't turn over', but as she said, they never turned over till they were turned out, so that was no

Chapter V

hardship. The fact that some sailors were being turned away did worry her. She had always told her helpers, 'NEVER turn a blue-jacket away, not if there is a corner for him to squeeze down in', but often there wasn't even that corner, and one night she was sadly amused when the night watchman said to her, 'Not even a windowsill vacant tonight Ma'm'.

Next to the Diamond Jubilee Block there was a public house known as *The French Maid.* It was such a lovely name, which conjured up the picture of the purity of Joan of Arc, with her incomparable bravery, and her implicit faith in the goodness of God, but the *French Maid* in Chandos Street was the antithesis of that, being one of the most ill-reputed public houses in the town. The small bar in the front led to a large dance hall. This was a snare for young men, while the women who frequented it found it very profitable. It was noted for bloody fights which started in the saloon and finished in the street; men fought bare-fisted, while women scratched and clawed with the result that blood and hair were strewn in the gutter. These brawls were so unspeakably horrid that even the magistrates felt their continuance reflected badly on the town's image, and refused to renew the licence when it elapsed. Their excuse was that the number of licences was excessive in that district and a reduction was desirable. Agnes heard the news thankfully and planned to buy the *French Maid,* complete with licence, but then it was rumoured that another publican had applied to take over the building in order to extend his business. Agnes Weston acted quickly: she bought the *Maid* for £1,300 contributing £300 from her own income. The *French Maid* was pulled down and in its place the Beresford Block was built to provide another 200 cabins. Agnes could look back with satisfaction: initially the Portsmouth Rest could sleep twenty men, but with the completion of the Beresford Block six hundred could be accommodated. When the huge building was complete it was certainly a Naval 'Hilton'. Cabins, as in Devonport, were sixpence a night and again, as in Devonport, by mid-day all tickets were sold.

The restaurant could compare favourably with the best cuisine that Portsmouth could offer. It was brilliantly lit by electricity, never closed, invitingly warm (as was the whole building) and must have been one of the very few to be completely centrally heated at that time. Because of the excellence of the food and the service, enormous quantities were consumed; each week-end an average of 1,700 sausages, 2,000 eggs, 3,000 rolls and butter, 2 cwt. of bacon, 5 cwt. of fish, besides bread, tarts, cakes, puddings and so on were eaten.

At one of the big open meetings at the Portsmouth Rest, Agnes Weston spoke first on the policy of the establishment and then Sophia Wintz gave the men a vivid picture of the size of her catering. 'Last year', she said, '378,375 men slept at the Rests and if they had linked hands they would stretch from Paddington to Plymouth, a distance of 245 miles. To feed them, and believe me you are great trenchermen, the animals eaten, oxen, pigs, sheep and so on, if put one behind the other would have been a mile long. The cocoa, coffee, and tea drunk during the last year would float a first-class torpedo boat'.

On entering the main door the men could leave anything of value, such as money or papers, with the receptionist who would lock it in the safe. There was a parcels office where goods could be deposited for any length of time and the owner knew that his property would be safe until claimed. There were several rooms for relaxation. Perhaps the most important was the reading room, which was kept quiet, and the well-stocked writing room, where the stationery was free; letters could be posted in the vestibule so there was no excuse not to write home. Next to this room was the 'Gentleman's Club' for a quiet smoke and a chat. The large billiard room and the small room set aside for chess were always popular. To see these rooms so well attended must have given Miss Weston much satisfaction for, not more than thirty years before, the rating was considered to be interested only in beer and loose living, but here was the new blue-jacket—her blue-jacket—evolving. In the recreation room was an electric piano and here community singing and concerts were frequent.

The basement, a self-contained unit, was the hub of the organisation. First there were the kitchens of which the overlord was a first-class chef attended by a large well-trained staff. They roasted enormous joints of beef, legs of mutton and pork, while in a separate room vegetables were prepared. In another section the washing-up was done and for this job alone four men were fully employed. Next was the enormous bakehouse with a staff of experienced bakers, who started work at 4 a.m. and made every item in the bread and confectionery line sold on the premises. Rolls were great favourites with the men, so there was always a plentiful supply of these and the favourite fillings were ham and cheese; thin sandwiches were rejected as shavings and trash.

A mineral-water plant had been installed and a potato-peeling machine—in fact everything possible to help the staff. This was a revolutionary idea for at the turn of the century domestic help was plentiful, and if one left there were ten after the job, but Miss Weston considered them as all important members of her team and not mere workers.

Away from the kitchens, but still in the basement, were the bath cubicles each containing a full-sized white glazed earthenware bath; hot and cold water was laid on and towels were warmed on radiators. A bath attendant was always on duty to see that all was ready for the men. Absolute cleanliness of baths and lavatories was of prime importance: all this in a town which as recently as 1847 had suffered a dreadful widespread outbreak of cholera which caused many deaths. Sanitation was then almost unknown and it was a common saying that in Gold Street gold would tarnish, in Silver Street shillings would turn blue, and in Copper Street the pennies would be covered with verdigris. The awful cholera scourge had forced the town's officials to take some action in providing better sanitation, but who would have dreamed that such amenities could have been provided as those in the Rests for the ratings? So much had been done so quickly. Near the bathrooms was the barber shop where the same high standard of hygiene was enforced. Visitors to the Rest declared that the degree of cleanliness and comfort provided there could not be surpassed in a first-class London club. The engine-room and boilers were also in the basement; huge boilers were needed to supply the gallons of hot water used in such an establishment. An engine of 125 horse-power worked the dynamos to produce electricity for the great building; thirty-five arc lamps illuminated the outside and the main parts of the building, while the rooms were lit by smaller bulbs. Miss Weston was proud to tell visitors whom she showed over the Rest that the wiring, 'if laid out straight', would extend for miles.

On the upper floors were tier upon tier of cabins, each one

satisfying the standard of cleanliness and comfort that Agnes considered worthy of her 'boys'. The whole building was patrolled by four night watchmen; the first rising-bell was just before 5 a.m. and a stentorian voice could be heard echoing along the corridors 'Show a leg, hurry up for the 5.30 boat'. Later this would be repeated for the 6.00 boat. The ships' officers knew that there was never any need for a man who had been staying at the Rest to be late. Sometimes there were 1,200 men wanting breakfast, and wanting it quickly.

Over a hundred staff were employed to keep the Rest running smoothly, and hours were kept to a minimum, an eight-to ten-hour day being the average; Miss Weston studied her staff and expected and got loyalty in return. Often she would say, with her heartwarming smile, 'We have always known how to haul on one rope'. If there was anyone with a 'growl' as she put it, she wanted to hear the 'growl' at once and then set about putting the matter right. A porter who thought the amount of food he was being given was inadequate took his luncheon plate to show Miss Weston. She thanked the man for pointing this out to her and by evening those in charge had been told that all the staff must have ample portions for no one who was not well fed could be expected to do a full day's work. There was no further criticism on the amounts served.

Agnes Weston was adamant that the ratings who went into the restaurant should not be in her own words 'preached at', so when she saw one of her helpers handing out tracts to the men she took the papers from the young lady and put them on the counter with a card saying 'Please take one'. This was quickly slipped to the sausage rolls, result plenty of tracts—no sausage rolls, but a very amused Miss Weston.

Many praised the Portsmouth Rest, but none more so than Robert Dolling who was priest-in-charge of St. Agatha's Church, Landport. He wrote that it was sad that the Church of England had no sailors' home,

> 'But,' he continues, 'if she fails there is one name that ought never to be mentioned without thanksgiving to Almighty God for her unceasing labour, and her truest and tenderest devotions to Jack ashore and afloat, the name of Agnes Weston. Her home, close to my parish, is worked on the most

admirable lines in all matters, excellent food, and sleeping accommodation, and above all personal kindness and sympathy. She has too a very bold and broad view of many measures by which the Service could be benefited, and a very able and willing tongue to express them either in public or in private, at drawing-room meetings or before a Committee of the House of Commons. Perhaps there is no one in England to whom the Nation owes a deeper debt of gratitude for a real elevation on the part of a most important factor in the nation's welfare and prosperity than to Miss Weston.'

VI

BY THE middle of the 19th century it was realised that if the ships were to be fully manned the Navy must be made more attractive to recruits. Up to the time of the Crimean War when men were needed to swell the number required to defend the country the hated measure of impressment had been used, but the mood of the country cautioned the government to abandon this form of recruitment. Like many other unpopular Acts, Parliament never abolished impressment, it was only suspended. It was not considered wrong to fight for one's country, far from it, but until comparatively recently, people thought of war as inevitable, and those who went to fight were heroes; those who objected were completely beyond the pale. Conscription used in the two World Wars was, in fact, only impressment on a national scale. It was not why it was done, but how it was done that was abhorrent to the people. Sometimes, the scenes were ugly and violent as on Devil's Acre and Mr. de Trotter, a naval surgeon, wrote in reference to the work of the press gang:

'The scenes of cruelty and affliction which have come under my review have wrung my heart a thousand times. They are not fit to be related for they exhibit all that is ferocious of war and disgusting in the policy of a country that can permit such a practice to continue.'

The *Hampshire Telegraph* (1809) describes a successful raid:

'There was a hot press on Tuesday night by which 500 seamen were obtained. At ten o'clock at night Captain Bonen assembled a party of marines with as much noise as possible

Chapter VI

to quell a pretended riot at Fort Monckton on the Gosport side of the harbour. As the news spread crowds ran to the fort to see what was going on, and when the captain saw he had obtained his object he silently placed a part of marines at the end of Haslar bridge, the only way out, and took every man who answered his purpose as he went to return home from the scene of the false alarm.'

Many public houses in the ports had hiding-places so that men could quickly outwit the impressers; the *Fountain* Inn had secret stairs in the thickness of the walls all the way from the bars to the top floor. By this route those evading the Press Gang often escaped. This was the same *Fountain* Inn that later in the century, Sarah Robinson turned into a comfortable soldiers' home.

Men who were impressed were taken without thought; there was no selection, it was a matter of getting someone, anyone. The result was a crew made up of unwilling men who were never likely to be shaped into efficient sailors. As can be imagined, it was often the slowest, mentally and physically, who were pressed and once on board these reluctant ratings had to be kept there, leave being reduced to a minimum to lessen the chance of desertion. Punishment was severe and was meted out for the slightest misdeed. Floggings were so frequent that it was said the men got hardened to the 'Cat' which, like impressment, was never abolished, but suspended in peacetime from 1871 and by 1879 in time of war. By then the new Navy was gradually evolving and it was considered by the Admiralty that the fear of corporal punishment would have a bad effect on the inflow of men to the modernised service. To look into the whole matter of recruitment for the lower deck the 'Manning Committee', was set up in 1850, and its report issued three years later. The measures recommended were introduced by Lord Aberdeen's ministry, and it was said that from this time the modern popular blue-jacket was born as the Committee brought the conditions of service for the Royal Navy rating in line with those for the Royal Naval officer. The report recommended that boy entrants should be employed continuously for ten years in the service after the age of eighteen, that a more educated type of lad should be encouraged to join, and if it was made known that the entrants could progress from boy to ordinary seaman as a matter of course it would encourage the type the Navy needed. But it was only after the second 'Manning Report' that the Navy was able to compete with the Merchant Service for suitable recruits as the second report introduced pensions after twenty years. If the blue-jacket began at eighteen, a pension at thirty-eight was something worth considering. A new rating of 'Leading Seaman' was introduced and there was encouragement by training and extra pay for those willing to specialise in gunnery. It was also made possible for any rating sufficiently ambitious to become a Petty Officer, and a new rank of Chief Petty Officer was created for the more efficient seaman.

With the introduction of the long-service sailor, it was important that he should have a uniform. The Admiralty thought it would raise the man's morale, while the surgeons hoped it would keep him cleaner and free from lice, which they were sure spread such plagues as the dreadful cholera scourge in the Crimea where the fighting force was decimated. Although sailors' uniforms were not standardised until 1857, the officers had enjoyed theirs for over a century. It was after the War of the Austrian Succession that a small band of young officers decided it was time they became organised, and formed themselves into a club. They met at Will's Coffee House in London whenever possible, and dined annually on St. George's Day. Their aim was to oppose all illegal innovations. They called their club the 'Amicable Marine Society', and declaring that they should have a uniform, drew by ballot the names of three men who should approach the King to ask for this. Captains Frankland, Spragge and Montague were appointed, and they put in their request to George II suggesting a uniform of red and blue, but according to the gossip of the time the King had so much admired the young Duchess of Bedford when he had seen her out riding in her dark blue and white rig that he decreed that his Royal Naval Officers should be uniformed in similar colours.

The ratings were for many years a motley crew; when their clothes were so filthy and lice infected that they had to be burnt then they could draw cloth from slop stores kept by the purser for coat, trousers and shirt which had to be made by the seamen themselves.

Some of the more wealthy captains, on the other hand, would dress the crew, or part of it, as they thought fit. Uniforms chosen by Captains make a fascinating study; one captain ignored his

Chapter VI 67

ill-clothed sailors, but bought expensive tall white beaver hats for all his officers including midshipmen and insisted that the hats should be worn at all times. The Captain of the *Blazer* dressed the boats' crew in blue and white striped guernseys, and vivid red coats, and is said to have originated the modern blazer. Commander Parry Wilmot, Captain of the *Harlequin,* dressed his gigs' crew as harlequins, perhaps only beaten in bizarrerie by the Captain of the *Wasp* who allowed his gigs' crew to grow beards and he added red caps to those 'hairy objects'.

In 1857 the first standard uniform was brought out and gradually developed until approved. A blue serge frock, later replaced by a tunic, a lighter blue collar edged with three white tapes not, according to modern historians, to commemorate Nelson's three great victories, bell-bottomed trousers, thick woollen jacket and a black silk neckerchief not worn in memory of Nelson but possibly as a sweat rag in time of war, and a protection for the coat from the grease on the hair in peacetime. The head gear was a straw hat, always worn on Sundays, or a cap, not originally bearing the name of the ship.

The sailor suit soon became very popular, not least because the Queen dressed the princes in miniature suits of the same design. She recorded in her diary, 'Bertie put on his sailor dress which was beautifully made by the man on board who makes the clothes of the sailors'.

Victoria also decreed that her sailors should have full beards or be clean shaven, 'Moustaches,' she said 'make them look like army men'. This order would not have pleased Admiral Sir Maurice Berkeley, who was so outraged when visited by the bearded Captain Moorsom, just back from an encounter in the Black Sea, that he shouted, pale with rage, 'Horse Guards next door!'

Thus it was only just over a century ago that the 'new blue-jacket' was born. Even so, it took several decades for him to become the familiar figure of the middle of the 20th century (since then in response to the dictates of the modern small but highly technological navy of today, there have been further, almost as far reaching, changes.) The Navy of the eighteen-sixties was still extremely hide-bound, steeped in almost a thousand years of tradition, for it was in 897 A.D. that Alfred had first mustered his small fleet of galleys at Spithead. Its views were ultraconservative, and it took a long time to absorb the changes in status recommended in the 'Manning Reports'.

It was with the development of this new seaman that Agnes Weston was so deeply concerned, and not only with the man, but with his wife too, for if Agnes was a mother of the blue-jackets, she was a devoted and dependable friend to their wives.

Many of the old sailors had never troubled to marry; they had kept one woman (or more) in port for their convenience, and when they went off, possibly for years, although the partnership had finished, illegitimate children were left behind. Agnes knew that such habits were dying quickly and she wrote: 'The blue-jacket of olden times is quickly passing and with the new sailor comes the new sailor's wife, the public will do well to purge their minds of Marryat's novels and look again at our modern Navy.'

The sailor's wage was too low on which to keep a wife and children, but, unlike the soldier, the blue-jacket could marry at any time without permission. When the husband was in port the family could just afford to live, but when he went on a foreign commission the family was often near starvation. Before the man went he had to 'kit up' and see that his uniform conformed to Naval standards of smartness and efficiency. His pay was changed from weekly to monthly, and two months' money was retained by the Admiralty in case the rating should 'run'. So often it was three months before the wife could begin to draw any half-pay, which was meagre enough when she did receive it. When Agnes started the Rests the sailor's monthly pay was £2. 8s. 9d. not a princely sum even considering the cheapness of food. Technically Jack, in time, got all the pay due to him, but until his wife could start drawing the allotment she and the children could starve. Miss Weston said, 'Many grimly remark that the blue-jacket, until he attains a higher rank has no business to marry, but whatever we do let us be human. If the pay of men of higher rank is sufficient for satisfactory family life, I told them that the pay of the lower ratings should be such that the wife and little ones should be supported with a little margin for a rainy day'.

Usually Agnes worked to a sound philosophy: if it was apparent that there was no prospect of moving the authorities to take a certain line of action she did not waste time on it, but concentrated on matters which would be fruitful. But over the three months' wait for the wives to draw half-pay she felt so strongly that she persevered until the Admiralty gave orders that the women could draw money at the end of the first month. It was a great triumph for Agnes, and the blue-jackets and their wives were deeply thankful to her, but she was still not satisfied with the arrangement and when an official called at the Devonport Rest to ask if the new order was working well to his surprise Miss Weston was anything but grateful, 'As far as it goes, it's alright,' she said, 'but how do they eat during that first month? I'll tell you, we help to feed many of the families here otherwise they would be starving'.

When it became obvious that the ratings' pay would not be increased Agnes decided to do three things. The first was to encourage the men to study and become better qualified, then to try for promotion or at least for badges which carried a little extra money; secondly she would endeavour to get the men to take their savings home; and thirdly she would make every effort to make the blue-jacket's wife's life a little easier.

The men had to have tuition to pass examinations, so Miss Weston set aside rooms for classes and quiet study. She then engaged first-rate instructors to teach the specialised subjects the men needed to learn. In one year alone 5,700 men took advantage of this free tuition, and a great majority passed their examinations. But all were not studious, and Jack's reputation for generosity and hard drinking persisted. In fact for years a sober sailor going back to his ship at night would pretend to be drunk in order not to lose face with his mates.

The time to encourage the men to take care of their money was when the ships were paying off. Often the men would wait for days before they actually received their money and then they would stuff the notes in their hats and be off. There were plenty eager to help them spend it and Agnes found the squandering of this hard-earned money on casual acquaintances pathetic, especially when it was so urgently needed at home. She consoled herself that things were getting better, for there were no longer scenes in the ports like the earlier occasion when a gang of men just paid off a ship engaged all the cabs they could get, and armed with jars of liquor set off to visit pub after pub. At each they drank, treated, re-filled the jars and then went off to the next one. Eventually only the horses were sober, the drivers and passengers being taken into custody. Perhaps one of the most stupid extravagencies was the sailor who wanted to show off to his mates, so put his five pound notes between bread, and ate his very expensive sandwich.

To encourage men to keep their money for the home Agnes opened savings accounts at the Rests. She also asked that the men should be able to buy their train tickets for home while they were still on the ship and that the trains should be ready as near to the docks as possible to transport the blue-jackets away. For some years the authorities felt this would infringe upon the men's liberty and be unacceptable. The male and the female outlook on this matter was so different: the male authority said, 'Jack has been a good lad for several years, now he wants a spree, who can blame him?' Agnes said, 'These men have been away for years, their wives have had a terrible struggle during that time, let them benefit now, don't fling the money away on the spongers who loaf around the docks'.

Ultimately Agnes Weston's persistence triumphed and great alterations were made in paying off the ships. Money could be transferred to any Post Office convenient to the drawer. Train tickets were taken on board and transport was as near to the ship as possible to get the men away. 'Such changes,' she said, 'such beneficial changes'.

But before this took place she tried to help the men keep their money for the right woman. Sometimes they were such spendthrifts that they begged their Mother Weston not to let them have a penny, but almost immediately after they would want to withdraw a large sum to go on the spree, as one told her when he wanted £5, but she gave him a pound, and with a twinkle in her eye said, 'And don't forget to bring back the change'. She tells of another seaman, who had never arrived home with more than a few shillings in his pocket, but then told her that he would like to take the £100 she was saving for him. Knowing that his wife would see little of this if he took it Agnes asked if she could send it direct, 'So much safer,' she added, and to her immense pleasure he agreed. After his leave he told her what happened. 'The house was all trim, and there were flowers in the sitting room, the kids were in their Sunday best, and there was a meal ready fit for a king. Well after that the Missus asked me what I had, and I turned out the few shillings from my pocket, and she was just going to start moaning when there was a knock at the door, and there I showed her the telegram for £100. You should have seen my old girl, never know the like. I bought her a silk dress, fit for an Admiral's wife, paid up her few debts. Then apprenticed the two eldest boys to trades, the rest I banked in the Post Office.' 'In whose name?' Agnes asked, hoping for the right answer, and it came, 'in hers, she's my Captain now'.

In money matters it was with the married men she was most concerned, but she was very grateful when a group of single men went to her and said, 'We call you Mother, then will you act like a mother to us, and draw our half-pay and take care of it while we are away?' This seemingly small request developed into a business big enough for a trained banker. She was custodian of their money and their business adviser. When on foreign service they would write to her for what they wanted and she would have the goods required sent out immediately. These were a rare mixture from razors to concertinas, and sewing machines to Nigger Minstrels' rig-outs. She said they wanted everything—even the improbable—and she did her best to see that they got it. About £84,000 of the men's money passed through her hands, and she would carry some £1,600 monthly from the Dockyard to bank it; she says she felt worth robbing, but never was. Year after year she endeavoured to induce the Admiralty to establish a Dockyard Savings bank and relieve her of this heavy responsibility, but the answer she repeatedly received was that the civilian Post Offices were sufficient. She knew that a Post Office on the spot was the answer and at last through her persuasive 'pressure' she gained her way and a Dockyard Post Office was established—it came to stay.

Much she would do for the lads, but when one sent her the following letter, she had to refuse his request:—

Dear Miss Weston,

I am coming home in about three months time, and I feel that I should like to settle down in life, and get a wife—but have no means of seeing any girl or getting to know what they are like. Will you look out a nice girl for me, if possible with fair hair, who will do for me? I send my photograph and

will marry her directly I come home. Will you please send me her photograph? I have known you ever since you came on the Impregnable when I was a boy, and I am sure you can do better than I can,
    and oblige your obedient servant,
                signed ...

Agnes's advice to the sender of this very naive letter was that he should join in some of the social activities at the Rest, and probably he would meet someone with whom he could settle. Mothers had great faith in Agnes Weston, and I have met more than one sailor's wife who told me, when she went to Devonport to marry, her mother instructed her, 'Go straight to Miss Weston and ask her to look after you until you are married,' and according to these women she never failed them. One blue-jacket took his wife along and asked Agnes to see that she was not lonely while he was away: she was seventeen and he nineteen, and was leaving just after their marriage. This one lonely young wife could be multiplied by hundreds. Agnes did her best to make their lives a little easier and more interesting. On Monday afternoons there was a meeting at each of the Rests to which all sailors' and marines' wives were invited, and usually there were between five and six hundred wives at each Rest. The babies were cared for in the crêche; the young children could not wait to get into the nurseries where there were plenty of toys, mattresses to tumble on, little beds to lie on and milk to drink. The crêches and the nurseries were supervised by trustworthy women. The halls were bright and cheerful. There was plenty of singing, a short Bible reading, and each week something of interest—a speaker or concert—anything to help the members was introduced, all tastes were catered for.

    The wives, helped by Agnes and Sophia, ran their own clubs, there were the Coal, Thrift, Boot and Drapery Clubs and, most important of all, the Sick Club. To help this society the wives organised various money-raising functions, none of which was as exciting as the annual bazaar. Agnes described in her diary one of these held in Devonport:

> 'It was a brillant success; the pretty stalls, dressed with flags, and named after various ships in the Royal Navy, were set off by our beautiful new hall. In the centre was a model ship, the "Agnes Weston", she was manned by children who dispensed

I JOINING THE ROYAL NAVY TEMPERANCE SOCIETY

II ROYAL SAILORS' REST, DEVONPORT, 1924

XII HOME, SWEET HOME

XI NIGHT SCHOOL AT THE PORTSMOUTH REST

XIII A SAILOR'S LIFE

XIV MY MOTHER

Chapter VI

penny gifts from its hold. The blue-jackets had a stall to themselves which they proudly called the H.M.S. "Conqueror" and I am bound to say took a considerable sum. The refreshment stall, the sweet stall, plain work, china, and flower stalls all contributed their quota. The bazaar was opened on the first day by the Right Hon. Countess of St. Germain, who spoke most kindly and warmly of our work, and of the interest she felt in it. As she ceased speaking the pennant of the model ship was hoisted and the band struck up the National Anthem. The bazaar was declared open. Our side shows answered very well, we had two-penny concerts, exhibitions of the cinematograph, hat trimming and washing competitions by blue-jackets and others, which created much merriment.

The evening of the second day was signalled by a jumble sale supervised by Miss Wintz, and when the hour of closing drew near the stalls were found to be empty, no raffling allowed, and the substantial sum of £203 taken. As the expenses were small the funds benefited considerably, so much so that a larger house was taken for the Holiday Home.'

The wives had had a holiday home at Saltash, Devonport—then a country area—where families could go for two weeks' holiday; the house, light and fuel were free. But the Committee did more than run the Holiday Home, important though it was, a portion of the funds being allocated to the Victoria Jubilee Nurses Association. The highly skilled nurses which formed this society were available for maternity work and general cases; by their affiliation to the Association the sailors' wives could have immediate attention. Pregnant wives were encouraged to try to save £1 towards the expenses which would accrue during their confinements. Agnes saw that a small sum from any profits of the Rests was added to each amount saved and her helpers stocked the cupboard with groceries to help the family over this difficult period; meanwhile the Secretary of the maternity committee engaged a nurse for the confinement. It was, Agnes said, 'one-big-help-one-another-society'. The Royal Sailors' Rest Needlework Guild was also most beneficial to the young wives of stokers and seamen. It was started by Agnes Weston who invited those with the means to contribute two or more garments a year to be sold very cheaply after the weekly meeting. Children's and babies' clothes were especially welcome. Some well-known person was invited to be President of the Society, often a member of the Royal Family, and when the Princess of Wales (later Queen Mary) was President she was personally very interested in the Guild and sent a box each Christmas containing her many contributions; in addition she would send a hamper full of toys and her husband always added his own generous contribution.

Agnes appealed very often in *Ashore and Afloat,* for toys either to use at the Rests or for individual families, but always added that the toys must be in perfect condition. This shows how differently she saw these blue-jackets' children from the way many affluent people saw the poor. If the toys were dirty, broken and not fit for the donor's children, then they were not fit for the blue-jackets' children either, and not wanted at the Rests.

Into the other clubs members were often able to put a few coppers; all the money was banked so that the interest although small could be divided among the savers. Sometimes the women saved for years to get a coveted possession. One old lady, now well over eighty, told me how she saved for so long to buy an eiderdown and at last had sufficient in the club to purchase one for thirty shillings. Her pride and excitement were great as she had never expected to own such a luxury; it was covered with yellow sateen, so beautiful and so wanted, and although it has been re-covered many times, it is still in use but it has never looked so beautiful as it did all those years ago. It is difficult to realise the acute poverty in which these women lived. Wives in the depression of the 'thirties were poor because their men were unemployed, but these sailors were fully employed, and often away fighting for their country while their families were constantly bordering on starvation; by many this was not considered at all unjust, or just not considered at all.

Branches of the Royal Naval Temperance Society and the Royal Naval Christian Union were formed for women, and each society boasted over 1,000 members. One sailor writing to Miss Weston said, 'The best thing you've done for a long time is to widen these societies for now we're all sailing in the same ship'. But it was not all savings and committee work for the wives who were members

Chapter VI 75

of societies at the Rests; in the summer there were outings which were days to remember. The children were left behind at the Rests and there no doubt given a very happy day so the mothers were quite carefree and had nothing to do but enjoy themselves. Sometimes the Portsmouth wives went to Portchester, a favourite spot, while the Devonport wives would be entertained at the Obelisk Fields. No packed picnic on those days: tables were laid with great care and the wives waited on by some of the staff from the Rests, while all were entertained by the Marine band. After lunch there were races which the ladies thoroughly enjoyed, despite tightly waisted skirts trailing to the ground, huge hats, and button boots. Flat races and three-legged races were the order of the day, and we are not surprised that there was no mention of obstacle races. A high tea was followed by a stroll in the fields, before home and a day to remember.

At Christmas there were parties for the children, and dancing and competitions for the sailors and their wives; tables were laden with food and presents for everyone specially selected to give particular pleasure to the receiver. The gift was always personal: if for the lady then for her alone and not for the home.

When Miss Weston first began her work with the wives she was saddened to see that the women had to go to the Dockyard to collect their allotment, or 'half-pay' as it was called. Often they had to walk miles to get there and take young children with them. If one was late she had to go another time on 'Recall Day'. Many times in winter the women were so overcome with exhaustion they fainted in the waiting room, while others were wet through and bitterly cold. The Rest was especially welcoming to them at those times as piping hot soup or tea was always ready which warmed them before their trudge home. The system was a relic of the old Navy and an unnecessary hardship to the women. Agnes Weston begged officials to alter this method of payment, but was met with stony refusal: this did not stop her from continuing to make it known how she felt about the distance the women had to go to collect their pay. At last she interested Sir Hudson Kearley, M.P., who brought the matter up in the House which decided to hold a Royal Commission at Devonport under Lord Farrer. This matter, which to 'My Lords' may have seemed so small, was vastly important to the sailors' wives. Miss Weston and Miss Wintz were called to give evidence, and in addition to this they sifted out evidence, and prepared witnesses for the Commissioners. At the eleventh hour Agnes and her friend had to keep up the morale of the witnesses who were so afraid of officialdom they wanted to flee, but Agnes was not going to let the Commissioners declare that the women were not interested and she saw that each gave evidence before she left the building. The result was the system was entirely altered and by 1895 every wife and mother receiving 'half-pay' was sent a monthly draft from the Admiralty which she could cash at the nearest Post Office.

Blue-jackets, wives and children were always welcome at the Rests but Agnes Weston had not planned any specific organisation for the young until she received several worried letters from fathers who knew that their sons were, as they put it, 'running wild', and becoming very disobedient and self-willed. The men were serving overseas and would be away for several years so they asked Miss Weston to arrange something to keep their lads in order. She called a party of her workers together and they felt sure that so-called naughtiness was possibly boredom. What to do with the boys was the question. Plenty of activity and something which connected them with their fathers' work was the suggestion, and so there came about the creation of the Boys' Naval Brigade. The boys were encouraged to join, they were provided with a smart uniform and there were many qualified instructors who volunteered to help with the work. The Brigade became enormously popular, and one company after another was formed. The Admiralty lent a seven-pounder gun for gun drill, and the boys were trained in such activities, as physical education, cricket, football, swimming, signalling and compass work; there were meetings uniting them all in temperance work, and Bible classes twice weekly. The Naval Brigade Boys' teams won many sporting matches. The Brigade was inspected by the Commodore of the Royal Naval Barracks and this Memorandum was sent to Miss Weston:—

> Royal Naval Barracks, Portsmouth.
>
> 'It gave me very great pleasure to see how well turned out and smart the companies field guns' crew and band of the Royal Sailors' Rest Boys' Brigade were, when inspected on 18th inst; and in my judgement this reflects the very greatest

credit on the commanding officers, the officers, instructors and all concerned.

A. Galloway, Commodore.'

Such commendation cheered the boys and those in charge of them. The certificates given to the lads who had trained regularly in the Brigade exempted them from some months training if they chose the Navy as a career. The girls were not going to be left out and formed their own Royal Naval Temperance Society. Connected with this were social gatherings, excursions into the country, ambulance instruction and regular Bible classes.

For the men who left the Navy and could not find work, and for blue-jackets' widows who were seeking employment, Agnes Weston opened an Employment Bureau, possibly one of the first in the country. In this way she hoped to be able to find suitable work for those in need, and often if the person required training for rehabilitation she would see that such training was given. Employers were eager to get personnel whom Miss Weston recommended.

So Agnes cared for the young, the wife, the sailor-husband, and the pensioner; and although this all took place many, many years before the famous Beveridge plan, there was a very comprehensive Welfare Service in operation at the Rests instigated and nurtured by Miss Agnes Weston, champion of the lower deck rating and his family, a true benefactor, and above all a practising Christian.

VII

LIFE WAS hard for the wife of a sailor, but much harder for the widow; as Father Dolling, who preached with such force on the shabby treatment of our service men, said ' ... and if the wife cries out and shames you, the sailor's widow, is without exception the greatest of England's disgraces'. When a ship sank allotments stopped immediately for the dependants of the drowned men. G.R. Sims wrote,

' 'Tis not only the husband that's missing,
'Tis the children's daily bread.'

The authorities could not envisage that in those little homes which suffered stoppage of pay there might be no money at all and often debts, especially if the husband had recently left this country, and had had the expense of 'kitting up'.

There were many dreadful disasters at sea during the fifty years which Agnes Weston worked among the sailors. In fact in the last half of the 19th century alone there were 49 ships lost in peacetime. Much of Agnes's time was devoted to relieving the widows' anxieties, and pressing all who would listen to help ensure a pension for the family if the sailor should lose his life.

She could have continued her mammoth work of running the Rests and caring for the blue-jackets and their families, and left the painful work of comforting the bereaved to others, but that was not her way. Her deep compassion for the suffering enfolded all who were in the need of it. When she had started in Mrs. Wintz's kitchen with the young sailor lads she little thought that one day her help would be sought nationally. Her first

Chapter VII

introduction to grief had been brought about by the loss of the *Eurydice*. Materially on that occasion, she had little to give, but spiritually she had much to offer. She prayed with the bereaved, and gave them such words of comfort as she hoped would help. In the little darkened rooms she found such sadness she never forgot, although she was to see similar scenes many times during her life. The families she visited in Portsmouth were desperately poor, yet mourning for all the relations had to be bought. This was a sign of respect to the dead and therefore obligatory. The wearing of black, and the crepe and weeds of the widows were familiar for years and it was only when clothes rationing was enforced in the Second World War that the buying of special garments for any occasion, even a funeral, became an impossibility.

Agnes was appalled by the dilatoriness of the Committees set up for the relief of the sailors' dependants, but their laissez-faire attitude seemed to be condoned by the authorities. Had these relief organisations been more efficient and prompt in action she might not have felt compelled to throw her energies into helping the destitute. Many years later she was generous when she was praised for her promptness with help, and replied, 'It is easy for us, we are a committee of two, and do not have to wait for the necessarily tardier agreement of a majority'.

On 8 November 1890, H.M.S. *Serpent* steamed out of Plymouth Sound bound for foreign service. She was a new cruiser and because all the latest improvements were included in her many were eager to join. Two nights after leaving England she crashed on a reef off Cape Trece on the north coast of Spain in pitch darkness. There was no panic: the officers grouped themselves together on the bridge; the men on the riggings or on the deck. The order was given for the boats to be lowered, but these capsized as soon as they reached the water. Then came the final order, 'Abandon ship'; the storm was so violent that only three men were able to save themselves. It was mainly a Plymouth crew and when the loss is centred in one area the tragedy seems so much more poignant, as when a great pit disaster means that practically everyone living in the district suffers some grief—or when a ship such as the *Hood* is sunk with its huge crew of which half may belong to one port.

After the news of the sinking of the *Serpent* the scenes in

Devonport were harrowing. Widows and mothers converged on the office of H.R.H. the Duke of Edinburgh who was then C-in-C; he was the second son of Queen Victoria and a most humane man. He saw with tears in his eyes the abject misery of the desolate women, several prostrate with grief while others fainted from exhaustion. Without delay the Admiral summoned Major Quill, the local secretary of the Soldiers' and Sailors' Families Association, Miss Weston and Miss Wintz with several of their helpers from the Rest. Steps were taken to trace all the bereaved and while this work was progressing the Sailors' Rest became a sanctuary to which mothers, widows and orphans went for help. If the blue-jacket's wife had received regular allotments made out to her she would receive a very small Greenwich pension, whilst for a mother who had previously received a regular allowance, there was the payment of a lump sum, but if the sailor had sent home at irregular intervals all the money he could spare, then his widow would get nothing from the Greenwich fund. If, however, the husband sent all he could afford home at regular intervals, but not through Service channels, then only if the widow could give absolute proof by his letters that he had sent money to maintain the home could she apply for the Greenwich pension. Proof was not always easy to provide and many a widow was left penniless because she had not preserved her husband's letters, which casts doubts on whether the regulations controlling the Greenwich Pension Fund were carefully explained to the blue-jackets before they went on overseas service.

The sinking of the *Serpent* happened so quickly. It seemed impossible that only a few days previously many of the lads had been eating, sleeping and attending meetings at the Devonport Rest and then, out of all the crew, only three survived. The Sailors' Rest helpers had been on the ship just before she left, and Agnes remembered, as she came away, a sailor was kissing his wife good-bye and saying, 'Cheer up Nell, take care of yourself and the kids, I'll be home soon'.

Public subscription poured in and the fund quickly reached £13,000. H.R.H. the Duke of Edinburgh, Major Quill and Miss Weston worked for weeks on the cases. Every family was discovered, every particular sifted out and arrangements made by which the whole fund should be used for those for whom it was intended. No expenses were taken. Wives and mothers were pensioned and a sum of money, invested at compound interest, laid aside for each child. Agnes Weston was unshakeably insistent here, as later, that the money subscribed to alleviate the hardships of the families of men who had lost their lives on the *Serpent*, should be used on that and that alone; not one penny should be put to any other cause or saved for some later date.

Agnes visited two of the survivors while they were in hospital and heard their stories. Three alive out of a crew of 176: no wonder Captain Marcus-Hare had written some years earlier his poem, 'There's sorrow at sea, sorrow at sea'. The two she met were Gould and Luxon, both very young and both badly maimed. Luxon, who was a member of the Sailors' Rest Temperance Society, grasped Miss Weston's hand and told her that after the order to abandon ship had been given he had jumped and being a powerful swimmer managed to get away from the vortex of the sinking vessel. She noticed that his arm was bent and asked if it had been injured. He modestly told her that he had kept a mate afloat until an enormous wave separated them and the other man was washed away; then he, Luxon, found his arm had stiffened. As she looked at his boyish face and realised the effort he had made to save his friend, she thought what heroes even the most humble of people are when the opportunity occurs; the useless arm seemed to be as great an honour as the V.C. She moved on to talk to Gould who had an equally dramatic story to tell, 'I never thought to see you again', he told her, 'but God has been very good to me; it's a miracle that I'm here at all, and it is God alone who has saved me. I was on watch, and I had my cork jacket on; I jumped into the sea I was whirled round like a top in the water, and then I sank, for the last time, or so I thought. All my past stood before me—all the good and all the evil that I had done and there was plenty of the latter. And then clear as a picture I saw my mother and she was praying for me; and I began to pray too, I prayed for pardon for my sins through the blood of Jesus Christ, and I prayed that He would save my life. In a minute or two I was carried against a rock: how I clung to it, and lifted myself out of the water, and how I thanked God for answering my prayer, as I held firmly to the rock the waves struck my legs with such force that I thought I was doomed to be drowned. How I prayed, for life is sweet to a man. Then the tide turned. I was saved. I took off my cork jacket and put in on the rock; then lying on it I slept from sheer exhaustion and must have slept for hours. When I awoke I had no power in my limbs at all, but by moving them gently I got a little life in them and at last I managed to crawl ashore'.

The Court of Enquiry on the loss of the *Serpent* found that an error of judgement on the part of those responsible for the navigation of the ship had occurred: she ought to have been on a more westerly course. Perhaps it might have been said that an error of judgement was responsible for the sinking of the *Tiger* during manoeuvres at night in total darkness. The ships were eighteen miles from St. Catherine's lighthouse off the Isle of Wight, and a mimic battle had just begun when the great hull of H.M.S. *Berwick* cut through the *Tiger*. The Commander went down with the ship, as did the officers and thirty-three men. Just as the sinking ship was making her final plunge the boilers burst thus increasing the horror of the sinking. All in the fore part and in the stoke-holds of the ship perished. Agnes Weston wrote in her diary that many good friends died that night including one of the gunners who had cycled from home that very day and called in for a chat at the Rest on his way to the ship. A similar accident occurred when the *Gala* was struck by the *Attentive* during the blackout of night manoeuvres in the North Sea, but fortunately then there was only one casualty, the Lieutenant-Engineer of the *Gala*.

After her relief work with the widows and mothers of the men who had lost their lives on the *Serpent,* Agnes established procedure which stood her in good stead for the many tragedies which followed. First she would send her helpers, or go herself, to visit and sympathise with the bereaved and see what could be done immediately to help. For those who lived far away from the Rests this contact was made through clergymen or social workers. Financial help was given as quickly as possible to tide the family over until permanent help could be arranged.

Agnes soon began her special National Disaster Fund and started it with her own substantial subscription. Funds began to come in from various sources, sometimes from fleets; the ships in the China Sea sent a contribution of £400 and others followed

Chapter VII

suit. These large sums of money were always accompanied by a formally polite letter from the Commander asking Miss Weston to add the enclosed to her fund, but had the men themselves written I am sure it would have been something like this:

'Dear Mother Weston,
   We are sending you this money collected from all of us, because we know that you will see it gets to the right people in time to be of use,
                    Your trusting blue-jacket sons.'

Sometimes it was a very modest sum from someone like the young officer just promoted who asked Miss Weston to accept his small donation saying that he wanted to give something as he was so grateful for all he had. Sometimes after a catastrophe the men would send to ask her to give help to a specific case as the men did from H.M.S. *Hart,* from which ship a leading stoker had fallen overboard and was drowned leaving two motherless children; the crew collected £42. 1*s*. 2*d*. to send to Miss Weston to use as she thought fit for the orphans.

Such stories could be told by the hundred of the generosity and kindness of the many for the sailors' widows and orphans for it seems that their pathetic state touched all hearts except those in authority. Much praise, however, must be given to the Mayors of the big ports who, time and again, had the painful task of making an appeal after a big naval tragedy.

Storms and gales continued to take their toll of ships and men, and in all cases the bereaved were cared for, initially at least, by Agnes Weston and her organisation. It is not the purpose of this book to advance reasons for the appalling loss of ships and crews, and the following is an account of only some of the actual disasters and the relief work which followed them. The *Gladiator* was going from Portland to Portsmouth at the end of April in weather more like mid-winter than Spring, with a blizzard blowing which reduced visibility to practically nil. In tremendous seas the *Gladiator* had just passed the Needles when she was rammed by the S.S. *Paul,* twice her tonnage and twice her speed. In less than twenty minutes the smaller ship had sunk. Many of her men were terribly injured by the impact and 26 were drowned. Miss Weston was asked for emergency help until official help by the authorities could be organised for the dependants.

The *Cobra,* too, was lost in a storm in the North Sea. The men had just taken over the torpedo boat from the builders' hands on Tyneside in October 1901. It was a violent sea; the ship battled through it all night but early next morning she suddenly collapsed and broke in two. The stem and stern shot up in the air, and in a few minutes the ship foundered; that morning there were seven out of sixty-seven left to return to their families.

Sometimes a ship was lost entirely and no one knew how. Such was the case when the *Atlanta,* employed on training service, sailed from Bermuda and was never heard of again. A reward was offered for any information, but it was never claimed; three hundred men were lost on that ship. There was a similar tragedy when the *Condor* completely vanished in 1900. She left Esquimalt on 2 December and was expected at Honolulu on the 15th, but had not arrived by 15 January, 1901. Then H.M.S. *Phaeton* was ordered to proceed from Esquimalt and follow the probable track of the missing ship; if any trace at all of the *Condor* could be found it was to be followed up without delay. The *Phaeton* made a thorough search and small pieces of wreckage were found with the name *Condor* on them, but no other sign of the ship was seen. One hundred and twenty lives were lost; the dependants refused to believe that their men had gone and for years were convinced that they had been washed up on some coral island and not been found. 'All I could do,' said Agnes, 'was to stand by and see that all were cared for, and none left out in the cold.'

The greatest peacetime tragedy came some years before the loss of the *Condor* or the *Cobra.* On 22 June 1893, a disaster never to be forgotten in naval annals was when H.M.S. *Victoria* foundered. The Mediterranean Fleet in all its glory was steaming along the coast of Syria, when a manoeuvre, known as the 'grid iron roll', was ordered by the Admiral, Sir George Tryon, K.C.B. This was to bring the fleet into suitable formation for anchoring as the vessels were going into Tripoli. The Admiral ordered that the ships should be six cables apart (1,200 yards) when the safety margin was understood to be eight cables (1,600 yards). It has been written that the Admiral, when holding an earlier command had contemplated carrying out similar manoeuvres which might have proved disastrous had not his senior officers refused to signal the command. In the case of the *Victoria* the order was semaphored

Chapter VII

and Rear-Admiral Markham, dubious of its correctness, had intended to signal his doubts to the Commander-in-Chief, but hesitated too long. At the Court of Enquiry it was regretted that the Rear-Admiral had not despatched his query instantly. Trying to carry out this manoeuvre a collision occurred which sent the *Victoria* to her doom. She was cut in half by the powerful ram of the *Camperdown* which was badly damaged but kept afloat. It was all so sudden, utterly unexpected, and dreadful. The ship's police on the *Victoria* took the prisoners up from the cells, doctors went to the aid of the sick while many of the crew stood in serried lines looking pale and anxious. Sir George Tryon refused the life-belt a coxwain offered him but told the man to save himself while there was a chance—unfortunately he was not able to do so. A brave young midshipman, Mr. Lanyon, said his place was by his Admiral, and he went down with the ship. An eye witness said that there was absolutely no panic. The Court of Inquiry praised the wonderful courage and calmness of the men and their excellent discipline. The witness continued that the men were all in their positions for hoisting out the boats or performing any duty that might have been ordered. The sailors on the forecastle worked with a will until the water was up to their waists, and it was only when they were ordered aft that they left their work to fall in on the upper deck. In the case of the men working below he said he was witness to their coolness and when the order was passed to go on deck there was no haste or hurry to desert the flat.

A great favourite on the *Victoria* was the chaplain, the Rev. S.D. Morris, a brave man, an earnest Christian, and a real friend to the ratings on the lower deck. A survivor wrote to Agnes Weston. 'We do miss our Chaplain'. The last time he was seen was trying to help rescue the sick and was heard to say, 'Steady then Steady—let me help you'. One of those ill at the time was Commander Jellicoe; he was suffering from fever, but jumped clear of the ship, and when he was picked up he found that his fever had left him. History might have been very different had he been one of the 21 officers who went down. As the *Victoria* sank the Admiral was heard to utter, 'It was my fault, my fault entirely'.

There is a strange story about this catastrophe told by Sir R. Bacon in his *Naval Scrap Book*. On the day that the *Victoria* was rammed and sunk by the *Camperdown,* he says, 'A number of torpedo officers, myself included, were lunching at the works of Messrs. Whitehead of Weymouth, where we had gone to witness some important torpedo trials. After lunch we were discussing the morning's work, when a wine glass that was standing on the table broke through the stem without anyone touching it. I forget who remarked, that this should mean a big naval disaster. Allowing for the difference in longitude, the glass broke just about the time the Admiral's ship was rammed'.

Eerie stories were often told about sinking ships. Because of their superstitious nature the sailors readily believed such tales, for there is a similar one told about the *Eurydice*. Captain Boyd Carpenter related how he was with Sir John Cowell, and Sir John MacNeill at Windsor when the latter suddenly exclaimed, 'Good heavens why don't they close the port holes and reef the topsails?' Sir John asked him what he meant and MacNeill answered that he hardly knew, but he saw a ship coming up the Channel in full sail with all the port holes open, while a heavy squall was descending upon her. This at the very time that a fatal storm fell upon the *Eurydice*.

With the heavy loss of 371 from the *Victoria* need for urgent relief was great. Pay-day for the men would have been a few days after the vessel sank; the money went down with the ship. Agnes saw the suffering and misery which brought back the harrowing memories of the scenes after the sinking of the *Serpent*. Widows and mothers crowded the Sailors' Rest at Portsmouth. It became a Government office, sending and receiving messages to and from the Admiralty as to the life or death of a son or husband. One poor mother who when she received the joyful news that owing to a misunderstanding because of a similarity of names her dear one was still alive, was so overcome with joy that the news nearly killed her. On Friday, 23 June, the day after the ship was lost, Agnes began to investigate the first cases and to give relief. One mother, although grief-stricken by the loss of her son, had the bailiffs at her door directly the news was known because of her arrears in rent; with the wage earner gone there was little hope of collecting the money. The woman was to be turned out. Miss Weston was soon there and paid off the debt; she could at least keep a roof over the poor woman's head.

A large meeting was convened by the Mayor in the Portsmouth

Town Hall and before a packed assembly Agnes eloquently pleaded for help for the widows and orphans. She said that with the help of God she would stand as far as she could between the bereaved ones and the want that was even then like the wolf baying at the doors. She started the fund with a personal gift of £500 and undertook to continue to give relief until it was taken over by an appointed Committee.

The fund quickly reached £2,788 1s. 5d. and ultimately rose to the staggering amount of £70,000. Such a response showed how deeply the general public felt for the naval men and their wives. Although feelings ran high; it was still many years before legislative insurance was introduced to safeguard widows.

In the days following the tragedy Agnes Weston had given financial help to a hundred families and the number soon increased. A depot was opened at the Rest for mourning to help cut down expenses for those who required black. Sophia Wintz said she was overcome by grief when women put on their weeds for the first time and realised the finality of it all.

Government pensions for those eligible were started in August 1893, but those of the Royal Patriotic Commission not till July 1894, a year and a month after the loss of the ship! Agnes Weston's own relief went on steadily until other help was available and then it closed to avoid overlapping. But she was as firm as ever in using everything contributed on the people for whom it was given, and she cleared out her special *Victoria* fund to the last halfpenny.

Public opinion forced an investigation into the dilatory working of the Patriotic Fund. Agnes was called as a witness and gladly gave evidence to a select Committee of the House of Commons. She took up many widows of the Crimean veterans who were in extreme distress. Some were in receipt of parish pay, while a large amount of money—many thousands of pounds of Crimean and other funds—was invested and only the interest used for the bereft. These old widows, all over seventy, gave their evidence in such strange surroundings with great self-possession, asking only that Miss Weston should remain by them. One old lady had been a nurse during the Crimean War, and had known and worked with Florence Nightingale, but despite her services in the field she was ruled out of benefit because she had married a month or two too late. 'Seems hard,' she said. 'I would have married sooner if I'd known it, but it does seem bad to live on 2/6d a week.' Another said that her husband had died for his country while she was starving for hers.

Theirs were pathetic stories but the Chartered Patriotic Commission took them on their lists and the old ladies rejoiced in the little extra help. Agnes Weston felt that this was a step in the right direction and as long as things were improving for those she cared for so deeply she would continue her work without undue criticism of others. Not so Father Dolling who was living in the Portsea area at the time of the sinking of the *Victoria*—and in his book *Ten Years in the Slums*—he made a scathing attack on the handling of charitable funds.

'Even when the nation's pity becomes universal', he wrote, 'and money flows in like water, as in the case of the *Victoria,* the charity of the nation is strangled by the red tape of officialdom. I, myself, prevented starvation to more than one house which should have been sacred to England and I believe that if it had not been for Miss Weston many would actually have died from starvation. The cruelty of the methods—they were actually contemplating using the police to make investigations—the tardiness of the relief given—they made Miss Weston's generosity an excuse; the niggardness of the pittance they doled out until public opinion forced them to increase it, should create a national scandal. The Commission has over and over again received money for a certain purpose and not used it, but rather hoarded it up. I thank God that I have been summoned to give evidence before a Parliamentary Commission, now enquiring into this soulless corporation, bereft of all bowels of compassion. The enormous sum of money given to its charge for providing for the wives and others dependent on the old Crimean warriors is so tied up that although at the death of every pensioner there will be a surplus of over £70,000, yet countless widows of Crimean soldiers, and even Crimean soldiers themselves are living and dying in the workhouse; and though some years ago £7,000 was released from its original trust, and they were enabled to apply this to pensions for those dependent on sailors and soldiers they never discovered one, although many

Chapter VII

are known to every man and woman in this country except the Commissioners. What one hopes to see is the creation of a new trust, which, by means of humane and competent Christian persons, should discover anyone who is entitled, by death of a relative, to help from any special fund. When these had been liberally dealt with the surplus should form a nucleus of a great pension fund for soldiers and sailors. From the liberality with which such appeals for the *Victoria* disaster were responded I have no doubt that the heart of England is perfectly sound on this question, above all let humane Christian hearts be channelled through which England's generosity pays back her debt to those who suffer so gallantly for her sake.'

Father Dolling was not the only person to express impatience at the almost studied indifference the Authorities adopted to the demand for adequate pensions. Sophia Wintz said, 'The men are eager to have a pension fund, and are willing even from their small pay to give towards it, so that the widow could receive 8/- a week, surely not too much to ask for a woman who has to bring up a family. A large grant would be needed but foreign governments provide such a fund, and we, who rely on the dependence of our navy should not be behind in such matters'. Here as so often we see the difference in the temperament of the two women. Something is blatantly wrong. Why isn't something done to put matters right? Why do we tolerate it? Impatiently Sophia wants reforms carried out quickly—no delay, no excuse. She finds it difficult to understand her friend's attitude, for if anything is unfair or wrong at the Rests then Agnes would have it put right immediately and the staff knew and respected her for it. But in matters concerning changes on a national scale Agnes was wiser for she knew that if there was to be a lasting improvement it would come slowly and she had faith that right would be done in the end. Feelings ran high in many quarters after the *Victoria* sank. *The Daily News* asked, 'Recklessness or Negligence?' Who was to blame? The Admiral certainly seemed to think he was culpable, yet in his biographies his recklessness or negligence is never stressed. Members of Parliament, for the moment, became very heated over the catastrophe, and one member urged that the widows of the drowned men of the *Victoria* should receive extra pension money. This suggestion was met with a furore of anger. Would the Honorable Member give more to the widows of the men who lost their lives at the sinking of the *Victoria* than to those whose husbands had died from wounds upon the battlefields? There was of course only one obvious answer, so the question of pensions for all widows was dropped.

There is a touching little story about a group of young women who attended St. Agatha's Church in Portsea. In 1892 they had their first outing as a club and had saved all the year for it. The effort had been well worthwhile and a beautiful day was spent on the Isle of Wight. They were therefore determined to repeat the excursion, but it was not to be for they felt in 1893 that others needed their money more than they needed their day's holiday and passed all they had saved over to the *Victoria* Fund. It was not only for National disasters that Miss Weston used her Fund so effectively; she helped those tragic individual cases which never made the headlines but nonetheless needed help. If a man was too ill to continue in the service he was discharged, sometimes with a small pension, but more often than not with nothing. He would perhaps spend some time in hospital and then be sent home to be cared for by a wife who was already living on her own wages which were a pittance to keep a home on and certainly insufficient to provide nourishment for her convalescent husband.

There were cases reported of ex-sailors slowly dying in the most impoverished conditions, in a single room without heat, where the bedding and the food were quite inadequate. All that could be done in many cases was to ease the lives until the end. Whenever Agnes learnt of instances of misery and deprivation she quickly allocated at least 10s. a week as a measure of alleviation. She was always conscious that there were many who were suffering unknown to her so she constantly asked in her own journal and in other Christian magazines to be informed of cases of ex-blue-jackets in need of help.

Tragedies in which the Navy was involved were not always caused by the sinking or wrecking of ships for sailors were often called upon to help others in distress on land. One such instance was when the Navy went to Sicily after the dreadful earthquake at Messina in December 1908. There among the havoc their courage and energy was marvelled at. Agnes said that she had never felt more proud of the men. She had detailed news of their work from letters. One officer wrote from the flagship, *Suryalus*

'We have had a time that I can never forget. I landed with a blue-jacket rescue party, and have seen, and what is worse, heard the wounded, who are buried under the ruins. We heard the cries of many whom it was impossible to rescue, and who were dying a slow death. Last night's experience I shall never forget; all night long we took charge of patients, women and children. The blue-jackets placed them on stretchers, bathed their faces, and did what they could to ease them. The sailors were so tender to the injured children that when eventually they were carried to the emergency hospitals the children clung to their sailor nurses and cried bitterly at the parting.'

The men of H.M.S. *Minerva* recorded the same terrible scenes, the dead piled four and even six feet deep in the streets, and children crying by the sides of beds on which lay corpses of mothers and fathers. In one street a poor woman rushed to them crying, 'Bambino, bambino,' and pointing to the top of a crumbling building. A British sailor climbed up, risking his life, only to find and bring down a little dead body. The Messina Deputy telegraphed from the town: 'The British sailors are working miracles, hundreds of persons owe their lives to them—All honour to the English heroes'. The sailors worked nobly with an utter disregard for self. Always patient and indefatigable, they spread an atmosphere of hope and cheerfulness around them. Their discipline and strength were as valuable to the despairing city and disorganised authorities as their practical service. An anecdote told of the men of the *Minerva* is worth recording. When the men and women were taken on board many scarcely had a rag to cover them and the distress of the women went to Jack's heart; great bales of serge were rolled out and with scissors, needles and thread, the handy men set to work and soon warm skirts were turned out and handed to the shivering women who did not know how to thank the sailors enough.

On one occasion during those terrible days King Victor met a party of British sailors carrying some injured Sicilians to hospital. He stopped and in fluent English expressed his admiration at the splendid discipline, organisation and energy displayed by the men.

From another friend who had just landed at Malta, after a spell at Messina, Agnes read words very dear to her:—

'You will have heard all about the City of Death before this arrives, so there is no need to give you an account of the sufferings of the poor people. Of the gallantry and unselfish work of your friends the British blue-jackets it would have done you good, though, could you have seen the way in which each man worked to aid and to nurse the poor suffering sick and wounded survivors; all toiled with devotion, and all scorned the thought of recompense or reward. Night and day the work went on of digging out the wounded and dead from the fallen debris, feeding the sick and hungry, and nursing the homeless children. Officers, doctors, seamen and marines all worked with one determination of assisting their fellow creatures,

Yours faithfully, C.F.'

This was one of the many hundreds of times that the Royal Navy went to the aid of those in distress after natural disasters. The discipline and courage of the sailors coupled with their kindness and compassion made the British Navy the most welcome of rescuers.

VIII

IT WAS not only natural disasters, but also the tragedy of wars which caused Agnes Weston much heartache. The British Empire had expanded so rapidly and was so extensive that inevitably there was nearly always fighting somewhere. A bid for freedom in the East, a full-scale revolt in the West, or a major war—no matter: whatever or wherever the trouble the Navy was always ready to meet it. For the Government and people recognised the Navy as the invincible defender of these Islands and never doubted its ability to do what was demanded of it in peace or war.

When the Crimean War broke out Agnes was still at school but said that she would never forget the wild excitement when war was declared against Russia. She recalled the cheers and the bands which accompanied men to their ports of embarkation, and the terrible privations they suffered in the Peninsula. Although she had no relations actively engaged in the fighting she followed the news with intense interest and sympathised with her friends who had fathers or brothers in the front line. Descriptions of the battles and the dreadful conditions under which they were fought filled Britain with horror; when one soldier said after a famous victory, 'What will they say in Britain now?' he would have been surprised at what they were saying in Britain, not about the victory but about the inadequacies of supplies for the men. *The Times* was quite fearless in its attack on the mismanagement of the war especially on the logistical side. Agnes found the war exciting and she and her friends worked hard to make warm garments for the men and rejoiced to think that they would soon be wearing the mittens, mufflers and helmets, but in later years she doubted if any of the comforts ever reached the men.

The Navy did not play a big part in the Crimean War, for most of the great battles were land battles; two fleets were engaged, one for the Mediterranean, and the other for the Baltic under Admiral Napier, who had great difficulty in getting seamen for his ships. When he appealed for help from the First Lord he was told to get what he could from this country, then to fill up with sailors from Norway, as they were good seamen, and as long as they were not put beside Swedish sailors they would be co-operative members of the crews: certainly not advice in the best Nelson tradition. But eventually the Baltic Fleet did set off to an inglorious campaign brightened only by the fact that among its men was the first naval V.C., Charles Lucas of the *Hecla* who saved many lives by throwing a live shell off the ship.

But Agnes at this time was interested in the Army and Navy only as fighting units. She never thought that fifty years of her life would be completely involved with the latter, but then of course it was many years after the end of the Crimean War that she became a declared Christian, and began the work she had been chosen to do. Quickly following on the Crimean War was the Indian Mutiny and in this Agnes did have a very personal interest as her two cousins were serving in the Army in India. Charles, when he returned to India from leave, was attached as a Lieutenant to the Naval Brigade, and posted with Captain Peel, who had recently won great honours fighting in the Crimean Peninsula. Charles Weston was inspired by the gallantry of the Naval Brigade and when he planned an expedition to take a fort he had the utmost faith in the men's efficiency. All went well until their officer was wounded; then they forgot their carefully arranged plans, crashed forward, stormed the fort, spiked the guns, took the rebels prisoners, carried their popular young lieutenant back to safety, and counted the night well done. 'Very brave, but a trifle over-enthusiastic,' was Charles Weston's description of the bluejackets. Captain Gould Hunter Weston, who was serving in India when the Mutiny broke out was sent to Lucknow where he served under General Lawrence, whom he loved as a father. Before the end of the siege General Lawrence died in the arms of Gould

Chapter VIII

Weston. Both of Agnes's cousins were mentioned in despatches, and Captain Gould Hunter Weston's son was later to follow his father's career and win honours in the Boer War, and was subsequently knighted for his services in the First World War.

By the outbreak of the Egyptian War, Agnes was much more in the centre of activities. She had been working among the blue-jackets for little over a decade, and knew many of the lads who sailed for Alexandria. Immediately hostilities broke out she organised helpers to collect and make comforts for the men. She sent books and magazines and, to all those who wanted one, a copy of the New Testament. Their letters told her what they wanted and she endeavoured to see that their wishes were granted. The men in Egypt were constantly in her thoughts and in her prayers.

Charles Beresford, whom she had first met in Devonport when he was flag lieutenant to Sir Harry Keppel, was in Egypt at this time. Agnes Weston and Charles Beresford were friends for many years, and in many ways they were much alike: both had the ability to lead, both were courageous, both like Nelson knew when to be able to ignore 'the signal', both were among those few who had the common touch and above all else both were devoted Christians. So when the daring Charles Beresford in his little gunboat audaciously braved the formidable guns of Fort Marabout, Agnes with everyone else in Britain was delighted. He had been ordered to wait patiently in the background in case reinforcements were needed, and to let the bigger ships attack first. Waiting was not Charles Beresford's strong point, and the night before the firing began he told his men that, if possible, they would 'have a go' on the following day, and 'have a go' they did. This touch of dare-devilry caught the public imagination, and on everyone's lips was 'Good old Charlie B.' 'Of course they like him', Agnes Weston wrote, 'he is the embodiment of what a British Naval Officer should be, he is brave and chivalrous'. Arabi Pasha, a colonel in the Egyptian Army, had imprisoned the Khedive in his own palace and declared that he would rid Egypt of foreign domination. So the British went to Alexandria to give their people safe conduct from the town. The famous teapot of the Naval Brigade which went all the way through the long campaign was named after this Arabi Pasha.

In the opening stages of the insurrection the masses were behind Arabi Pasha to a man, but gradually as his guns were put out of action he found himself practically deserted. Into the chaos of Alexandria Charles Beresford, with a party of 130 sailors and marines, was detailed to land but to act more as a police force than a fighting unit. He quickly organised his men into gangs and set about restoring order. Each party was responsible for a special duty, one dealt with fires, a second was the burial party, another cleared the debris, and soon the town was habitable again.

Agnes Weston was so proud of 'her boys' that she treasured up all the news and praise of them she found in the papers, and when the wounded came back to hospital she visited them regularly and was never tired of hearing their adventures. There was one incident she retold many times. A party of blue-jackets, certainly not engineers, were taken to mend a part of the lining of the wall of a canal, the water being essential to the population of the nearby town. When the job was finished the men asked for ten minutes stand easy, this was readily granted and before they fell in to march back to headquarters they had erected a board on which was boldly printed, 'THIS IS THE WALL THAT JACK BUILT'.

One wounded sailor told her of the rule Captain Beresford made about looting, that whatever the men wanted a fair price had to be paid. When he saw a blue-jacket having much trouble to salute and hold his tunic down at the same time, said, 'What are you trying to hide?' 'Nothing Sir.' 'You've been looting, out with it.' A convulsive movement revealed the tail feathers of a cockerel, and sadly the blue-jacket pulled the bird out. 'Sir,' said the rating in defence, 'I told him three times to crow for England, and he never made a sound, so I'm taking him under arrest!'

It was a long campaign, but all the time the Naval Brigade was overseas Agnes saw personally that the men were supplied with all of the comforts which could be sent.

At the close of Victoria's reign came another major war, in which a firm stand was made against the Boers in South Africa. Strange as it may seem now, there was overwhelming enthusiasm for it. Volunteers rushed to enlist, and everywhere could be heard the strains of 'We're the soldiers of the Queen', which was the battle hymn of the time. It turned out to be a savage war fought in a country few Britishers knew and one wonders what inspired such

Chapter VIII

an upsurge of patriotism. Perhaps it was due to the high esteem in which the Queen was held, or more likely because in 1899 to the average British man-in-the-street the Empire stood for security. It was his own very special world, and nothing, if he could prevent it, was going to destroy the British Empire. Whatever the cause, the desire to fight an enemy 6,000 miles away was genuine, for we read of men who were rejected weeping unrestrainedly as they left the recruiting centres, and those ill in hospital praying to get better so they could go out and fight. The Royal Navy was to the fore and Agnes Weston knew many of the men who went, members of the Christian Union and the many who were her friends and who made the Rests their second home. She realised that hundreds would never come back and from sad experience was aware of the heartbreak there would be when so many wives were widowed and children made fatherless. For these sad events to come she tried to prepare herself. When R.M.S. *Briton* was due to sail from Southampton carrying hundreds of blue-jackets to South Africa she and Sophia went to the port to say goodbye to them. It was a miserable wet November day. Everything was depressing, not least the news from the Cape. The Captain invited the ladies on board and Agnes spoke to the men: 'You go to fight your country's battles, I stay here to keep in touch with your wives and mothers, and if anything should happen to you, to stand by them in your stead, which with God's help I will do'. She shook hands with as many as possible, then left the ship, but watched them as they manned the riggings and gave three cheers for the Rests, and as the gap widened between land and ship they broke out into the most melodic of all war songs, 'Say au-revoir, but not good-bye'. It was a parting she was not likely to forget.

The men of the Royal Navy and the Royal Marines took their places to fight side by side with the soldiers. H.M.S. *Terrible* and H.M.S. *Powerful* which were both diverted and sent to the Cape, were the largest vessels of their kind built for the Royal Navy, in the 19th century. Each landed a thousand men as reinforcements. Percy Scott, Captain of the *Terrible,* was convinced that the British forces would need siege guns; all they had were field guns, and with the main base thousands of miles away supplies were not easily obtainable. He had 12-pounder guns mounted on huge logs of wood, and bolted to bases. It seemed as if Captain Scott's instincts were prophetic for almost before the job was finished General White telegraphed from Ladysmith to Rear Admiral Harris, Commander in Chief at the Cape, to know if the Royal Navy could send him some 4.7 guns to keep the Boer artillery in check. By five o'clock, on the day the request arrived, the *Powerful* was taking the guns to Durban, and from there they were drawn overland to Ladysmith. They reached the town just before it was beleaguered for 119 dreadful days. The only news out was carried by pigeon. At the beginning of the siege the Governor of Durban became more than apprehensive about his town's fate and appealed to the Navy for help. Men from the *Terrible* and *Powerful* were scattered to towns whose survival depended on these reinforcements. A very appreciative description of the Naval Brigade's work at Ladysmith is given by the war correspondent G.W. Steevens, in his book, *From Capetown to Ladysmith,* unfortunately this book was never finished because its author caught typhoid just at the end of the siege and although he weathered the fever he took insufficient care of himself and died from a heart attack during convalescence. Before his death he wrote at length and with admiration of the men of the Naval Brigade. So many things about them he found commendable, not least their ability to make themselves at home in the most unusual surroundings. Their camp was spick and span, there were books and magazines for all, 'Who else', asks George Steevens, 'would have brought reading matter to a siege except the Navy?' All the men went on watches, bells rang out the duty, the camp might well have been a cruiser lifted from the ocean and planted up country. The guns were named, mostly after royalty, and the names carefully outlined with gold leaf. Did they, the war correspondent wanted to know, bring this especially to decorate the names or did they carry everything possible that they might need? The men added their own messages by the guns: by the side of one was printed, 'Who sup with me require a Devil of a long spoon'.

One afternoon when the Captain was entertaining Mr. Steevens the enemy was being very active. There was no panic. 'We'll go up if he fires again', said the Captain and when the firing restarted they made their way slowly towards the 'conning tower'. As they passed through the camp the men lined up trimly. Such natural discipline, and after five weeks in a besieged city!. When they reached the 'tower', the Captain waved his stick towards Surprise Hill. 'That man shooting is a German, and a German atheist at that, no one but a German atheist would have fired at us at breakfast, lunch and dinner on the same Sunday. Sunday, too, but when a shot went only ten yards from our cook then it was time to retaliate, we could spare anyone else but not the cook.'

The men in the Naval Brigade were delighted to be in South Africa. 'All I wanted to do was to get home', said Steevens, 'then I realised the blue-jackets had already been away for over two years, and it would be a long time before they would see England again, but they considered this spell a holiday'.

'Of course we enjoy it', they would say, almost apologising for saving the civilians, 'we so seldom get the chance'. Almost the last words that Steevens wrote were, 'The Royal Navy is the salt of the sea, and the salt of the earth too'.

Another correspondent from Cape Frere wrote home: 'The Naval Brigade is simply invaluable. Officers and men have won the warm regard of everyone in the camp. What particularly excites enthusiasm is the cheerfulness of the blue-jackets and their tireless endurance of hardship and danger'.

By common consent the bravest of the brave were the Royal Marines at the Battle of Graspan, and when Agnes visited the wounded who had arrived home, she heard their story at first hand. 'It was a warm 'un and no mistake, we swarmed up at dead of night, unsuspecting and my word how they peppered us, opening fire at 1,000 yards. We wheeled round right, then some wheeled left. I was in that company, here we left our Commander, shot through the heart. Yes, and Midshipman Huddart, there's stuff for you just a boy, shot three times and up again with the best of them till he dropped. I don't think we've changed much since Nelson's days. At 200 yards we fixed our bayonets and charged. We first saw their heels, they didn't wait when they heard the rattle.'

During the entire war and actually for several months after the fighting had ceased Agnes Weston was organising the great cases full of comforts sent from the Rests. Altogether more than £4,000 worth of goods were despatched to South Africa.

During the fighting and as Christmas approached Agnes thought that if each man of the Naval Brigade had a Christmas pudding it would remind him of home. Peek, Frean and Co. carried out the order and 1,300 1 lb. puddings, each in an air-tight tin with key to open it, and the message, 'With Miss Weston's Best Wishes' was sent to every man and they reached the front just in time for Christmas.

A bronzed blue-jacket when he returned told her, 'Directly Ladysmith was relieved we were outside the gates, and those puddings tasted just splendid after so many meals of mealies and mule flesh'. In addition to the puddings Agnes sent 1,300 1 lb. tins of Navy Cut and 1,300 briar wood pipes for the men. The Queen sent a box of chocolates for each man, these too arrived on Christmas Day. A blue-jacket, months later, told Agnes, 'Aye, I got the Queen's box, and still got it too, and the stuff inside. It was very difficult to keep it sometimes when rations were short, but I always minded who it came from'.

When the *Powerful* eventually came home the beaches were thick with cheering crowds, while mothers and wives hurried to the ship to welcome home their men. Agnes Weston went aboard to greet her blue-jacket friends and saw even on that one ship the toll the war had taken. Some of the men were bronzed and healthy, but far more were pale and ill from enteric fever, and many wounded were still bandaged. In a country that quickly forgot its heroes she wondered what their future would be.

Gradually the service men returned, but until the last contingent was back Agnes saw that crates of socks, handkerchiefs, shirts, lozenges, chocolate, Bovril, books, writing paper, Bibles and hymn books were sent regularly with copies of the wartime *Ashore and Afloat,* designed especially for the soldiers and sailors.

If Agnes had known sadness during her many years with the blue-jackets, her full sorrow came with the First World War. Then 74 years of age, she had known so many young men go to war never to return, and now once more great toll was to be taken. No one in 1914 could possibly have imagined what that toll would be. Agnes had felt so close to the Germans; she knew German officers and men personally having entertained them at the Rests, and she had been proud to see British and German ships side by side at Reviews at Spithead. The German Royal family had always taken an interest in her work and been generous with subscriptions. The

Chapter VIII

Germans had started sailors' homes, modelled on the Rests, in all their major ports. Now after being such close friends they were enemies and those who had fraternised only a few years before at the Rests would be slaughtering each other.

In the ports the war started dramatically as the Marine buglers stood on the street corners calling the men to mobilise. The Rests became centres of enormous activity; troops flocked to them and for the first time soldiers were welcomed there by the sailors as brothers in arms.

Optimists in the Government as well as among the general public at first prophesied that the war would be over, with an allied victory, in a matter of months. But it dragged on and on, with all its misery and slaughter, for nearly five years.

For the workers at the Rests it was a time of toil and tears; the flow of men was unending with so many going off never to return. Food became scarcer and scarcer, and Sophia fought a constant battle on the home front to get sufficient food to feed the hungry hordes. In the ports where Agnes and Sophia were working the grief was always round them; much of their time was spent comforting the sorrowing. After Jutland it seemed that nothing could ever be so terrible again: Agnes sent out five thousand letters of sympathy. There were so many women widowed in Portsmouth that the memorial service was held in Victoria Park because of the large number of mourners. In one street alone there were forty widows after the battle. Only hope and prayer kept the people going in those dreadful years.

Agnes Weston never sought publicity and rarely talked of herself, but in September 1917 she gave one of her very rare interviews to the *Western Mercury*. The journalist wrote,

> 'The door opened and Miss Weston came forward with a smile on her lips. She looked in perfect health, and an hour's talk with her revealed no signs of weariness in the great work in which she had so long devoted herself. When I asked her if she contemplated giving up she looked amazed "Give up", she echoed, "I pray to God I will stick to my post to the end. Sometimes", she continued reflectively, "I am reminded by my friends that I am getting older—no, no matter what my age is, that doesn't matter, a woman is as old as she feels, please ignore my appearance, I feel twenty-five". Then she

laughed her sweet silvery laugh which the sailors know so well. In the beautiful hall at the end of the corridor a cinematograph show was being enjoyed by both soldiers and sailors. I mentioned to Miss Weston that there seemed to be a splendid comradeship between the forces, and she replied "Yes, they are no longer rivals, they are brothers-in-arms. In the old days the sailor would not mix with the soldier, but all that has changed and now they fraternise most admirably. The folly I hope has gone for ever". Then she went on to give me the returns relating to the number of combatants catered for, from the outbreak of war. During the three years beds at Devonport and Portsmouth for the fighting men had numbered 1,396,150—hot baths 258,298—hot meals at 6d. per head 18,130,800—attendance at smoking concerts, 541,267—attendance at devotional meetings, 95,681—games of billiards played, 122,804—woollens given away 111,869—letters written and posted at the Rests, (stationery provided gratuitously) 290,422—visits to hospitals, 1,407. Miss Weston spoke with the burning passion of a veteran reformer, it is the breath of life to her. "We live in the premises", she said alluding to Miss Wintz, herself and also to her other helpers, Miss Peters and Miss Sharpe, "because unless that is done you cannot make a real home of it. The men like to see us about. They tell us it takes a woman to make a home and of course they are quite right. We can never do too much for these brave fellows. Think of what the sailors are doing for us and try to picture the plight of this country but for them, and I mean the Merchant Jack as well as the blue-jacket. Let me give you a few illustrations of their extraordinary spirit:— When H.M.S. ... came in after being torpedoed three times, men arrived in all rigs, singing and laughing. They had had a bad time but they went back to sea as soon as they could get *kitted-up,* some even forfeiting their leave so that they might be back in the thick of it immediately. The crew of a mine sweeper floated and swam for nine hours. They were described by their rescuers as having not a stitch on, except one man who had an oil-skin buttoned around the neck. Yet they were cheerful and bright and several rejoined within twenty-four hours of rescue.

An oil ship was torpedoed off ....., the crew was pitched into a sea of oil, one of the men had a broken thigh, he has since recovered and rejoined. Others went back the day after they had been torpedoed. Asked if they had not had enough they answered "'If we don't do it some one else must'". Isn't it glorious to witness the fortitude and self-sacrifice of these brave men? No word of fear, no word of apprehension, no thought of self."

Miss Weston told me of the Women's Guild, two thousand strong, but her face hardened as she recalled some of the unkind things said about sailors' wives, as a class she considers they are grossly maligned. "There are", she continued, "painful cases" (who should know better than she), "but as a whole they are women of whom their blue-jacket husbands may be justly proud". She met the charge of thriftlessness by pointing to the success of the savings bank which is run at the Rests, and £2,000 had been accumulated in the first eight months of this year, all in small sums.

"Some times I sit by the window and think over the past" Miss Weston said thoughtfully. "In the old days some of the scenes in the Rest and outside were terrible, running fights engaged in by men maddened by drink, and often fists crossed before my face as I stepped between them, poor fellows. We never got at them, but talked to them as their mother would have done, and many of the men have told me that it was because of the treatment they received here they decided to let drink alone. The Navy has altered immensely. The blue-jackets I met when my work was in its infancy possessed magnificent qualities, but they had not had the advantage of education enjoyed by men of the present fleet. Total abstinence with education has made big strides. Now I know of no class of men more temperate than the blue-jackets. But there I could go on talking and talking about them, aren't they splendid fellows?" '

In the whole hour's interview never once did she mention her own great loss which had been so recent and which had cut so deeply. For in 1917 her younger nephew, whom she loved as a son had joined up, and within four months had died from head wounds. During his childhood, Jack had lived at 'Ensleigh', gone to prep school at Bath, and then to Malvern and from there to King's College, Cambridge. When Mrs. Weston died, as Jack's parents were constantly abroad, he spent his vacations with his aunts. Sometimes in termtime Agnes would go to Cambridge, a town which she liked very much, to visit him. It is only when she writes of how delightful it was to have him with her on holiday at Waterlooville or at Grayshott and how refreshing it was to hold long discussions with him do we realise that she had any private life at all. She said it was the day of days when she watched the ceremony at which he took his B.A. degree. On leaving Cambridge, Jack's life somewhat changed. He had been destined for the Church, but did not think himself good enough to teach others and commenced a life of self-denial in London among the poor and downtrodden. He worked first with the Cambridge Settlement and then with the Charity Organisation Society in London where he was much loved and respected. If his Aunt Agnes was disappointed that he did not enter a theological college directly he left Cambridge she certainly never showed it, and I am sure that he must have been greatly influenced by her, following her lead in wanting to help the outcasts of society. The people loved him and he loved his work, and he carried on year after year never tiring, broken only by a few walking tours in Switzerland and France. Agnes says, 'I can truly say that he never gave us an anxious moment, but then he was one who thought but little of himself'.

His Aunt Agnes and his dear Aunt Sophie (as he lovingly called Miss Wintz) were convinced that when they died everything connected with the work at the Royal Sailors' Rests would be carried on exactly as before, or even improved upon, by Jack Weston. His elder brother, Charles, was already commissioned in the Army when the war broke out, and was certainly not expected to dedicate himself to his aunt's work, but it was he who eventually carried on the work and did so very successfully.

Jack felt that he must join the Army, and enlisted in the Queen's Westminster Rifles. He was sent for training at Hozeley Down, from where he wrote many amusing letters of the ups and downs of a soldier's life. Jack (like his Aunt Sophie) liked gardening, especially the cultivation of flowers, and round his hut at Hozeley Down his garden was the envy of all, but when, according to his letters, he was moved to other quarters the garden was given over to others. Later when he was in France he wrote to his Aunt Agnes to tell her of the pleasure he had when he saw whole areas covered with golden dandelions, and that in a derelict garden he found forget-me-nots and narcissis which he picked to decorate the mess table.

But at Christmas 1916 he was still in England and he spent the last Sunday of the Old Year at the Rest and was present at a crowded Watch Night Service. When it closed one of the most earnest workers, an ex-Royal yachtsman who had known Jack from boy-hood said as he took his hand to bid him good-bye, 'Mr. Jack, Sir, have you taken the Lord Jesus Christ as your personal Saviour?' Very quietly, but very firmly Jack answered, 'Thank God I have'.

In February 1917 embarkation orders came and he wrote to his aunt: 'I fear it is quite impossible for me to come down to say good-bye, much as I should like to have done so. Still our affection does not need the stimulus of such meetings to keep it alive. I go out feeling God has been extraordinarily good to me all my life, Your loving, Jack'. This letter was written on 25 February 1917, and her answer went off the following day.

'My dearest Jack,

I am not going to bother you with a long letter, but my deepest and undying love will go with you everywhere—there is really no good-bye between us, you have your life and your duty to do and may God bless you in it; in all probability I shall go first and I shall look out for you at the right time on the other side—you will always have had my prayers and I need not tell you how thankful I have been to see that you have taken the Lord Jesus Christ as your personal Saviour, as I did many years ago—I am sending you a little book that I use every morning, in addition to my personal prayer, and if you will use it sometimes I shall feel that we meet—so I say to you as one of old did, "Go and God be with you,"

Your loving aunt,
Agnes Weston.'

By March Jack was waiting to go to the front line, and when his aunt asked him if he needed money or anything else she could send him he replied,

'You kindly ask me if I need anything, actually I don't and as for money, I am passing rich in that I have sufficient for my needs, and I have not yet spent the £50 you so generously bestowed upon me a little while ago. How can I accept any more until that is exhausted. You have so many more satisfactory means of spending your money than on a doubtfully satisfactory nephew ... '.

He gave his aunt graphic descriptions of the life he led in France and his first stay in the trenches. It was not nearly as bad as he had anticipated. He had dreaded the noise of the guns and the shells, but the reality was not so terrifying as the anticipation had been. During a few days' respite behind the lines he was appalled by the France he saw. 'I could not believe,' he wrote, 'that such desolation was possible if I had not seen it—shell holes every few feet, not a tree that was not broken and splintered, the ground pitted by shells in every direction, and the whole countryside hopelessly blasted. We stayed in this little town, which was a heap of ruins and we bivouacked amid all the rubble, and remained in the holes and cellars for two days'.

When the men were short of comforts Jack sent an S.O.S. to his aunt, who saw that supplies were despatched promptly. When he received 100 pairs of socks, 50 pairs of gloves, 50 pairs of mittens and 100 writing pads he wrote immediately to her, 'What riches! Following your lead I shall disperse these things at once; there is no blessing in hoarding, and on active service it would be impossible'.

His cousin, Sir Aylmer Hunter-Weston, sent to Jack to say that he had planned a meeting directly Jack could get a few days' leave, and he wrote in his letter the following praise which Jack sent back to his aunt.—'Please give my kindest remembrances to that magnificent woman Miss A.E. Weston for whom I have so high an admiration and regard. If everyone of us were able to do a tithe of the good she has done this world would be a much better place than it is'.

Their meeting never took place, for by mid-May Jack was back in the trenches, where his spell of active service then was pathetically short, for on 21 May he received severe head wounds, and after two major operations from which he scarcely regained consciousness he died on 6 June.

Chapter VIII

In *Ashore and Afloat* Agnes Weston wrote of her nephew's life and death. It is easy to share one's pleasure with others, but she needed great courage to share her deepest sorrow with her readers. She wrote at the end of the account: 'I have been called upon to pass through very deep sorrow in the loss of my nephew John Cecil Weston, as dear as a son to me, and I can truly say I have given of my best and dearest'.

IX

A VERY important branch of Agnes Weston's work became the promotion of good relations between Britain and other countries through hospitality to visiting foreign fleets, for after the accession of Edward VII ships from other countries visited Britain far more frequently than during Victoria's reign. Many of these visits were in return for calls made by British ships; others were mostly courtesy visits after King Edward VII, 'the apostle of peace', as Agnes called him, had travelled from country to country offering friendship and goodwill. For Edward's Coronation in 1902 ships from a dozen countries gathered at Spithead and stretched in a magnificent fifteen mile long line of strength. When the King's sudden illness caused a postponement of the ceremony, these ships sailed quietly home after their brief stay, and only the men of the Japanese ships became acquainted with Miss Weston on that occasion.

In charge of the Japanese ships in the Solent, was Admiral Gore Inguin who was a Christian, as were three of his captains. He asked permission for a party of his seamen to go to the Rest at Portsmouth to see how it was organised with a view to opening similar 'clubs' in Japan. The Japanese were ever alert to increase their efficiency and were fully aware of the inestimable value to the British blue-jacket of the Royal Sailors' Rests.

Twenty Japanese sailors with a warrant officer were welcomed to the Rest. First, that most welcoming item of all—food. They had a very good supper and then Agnes Weston and Sophia Wintz talked to them. Fortunately a Japanese traveller was staying in the town and was happy to act as interpreter. After the meal and the greetings there was a comprehensive tour of the Rest and their many questions answered, so that the visitors saw exactly how every section of it was managed. Each sailor was given a cabin for the night, and the next morning, after a hearty breakfast, the Japanese returned to their ship, convinced of the comfort of the Rest. Within twenty-four hours the ships left for home, but before sailing Admiral Gore Inguin sent Agnes a beautiful bronze bowl ornamented with tortoises. She had few personal treasures, but this was one of them. The tortoises, the donor said, were symbolic for tortoises lived for two hundred years, and he hoped Miss Weston might do likewise. For the Rest she received a cheque for five pounds to be spent as she wished, and with the cheque was a charming letter of thanks from the entire party whom she had so happily entertained.

This had been but a brief encounter, but Agnes felt that the two navies had much in common, and of course for many years our sailors and marines always looked forward to calling into any of the Japanese ports for there they were welcomed and fêted and were so popular that great hospitality was offered them.

In 1906 two Japanese warships the *Katori* and the *Kashima*, made a longer stay at Portsmouth. As they berthed the helpers from the Rest went aboard to welcome the men and to invite them to a reception at the Royal Sailors' Rest. On the appointed day the men were headed through Portsmouth by the band of H.M.S. *Excellent*. They were met by Agnes Weston and Sophia Wintz, with three interpreters, one of whom was a Japanese clergyman studying in England, and the other two English—the Reverend Charles Warren, a C.M.S. missionary home on furlough and Miss Ballard, who had lived many years in Japan, and spoke the language like a native. Tea was served, and it was a tea which only the experienced caterers of the Rests could provide for hundreds of hungry men. This was followed by an address of welcome. Then came songs and displays of dancing by local schoolchildren. Before the sailors left Miss Ballard stressed the point that while they were in town they were to look on the Rest as their meeting place, somewhere at which they could always find a friend, or perhaps to write their letters home, for it would be somewhere where they would always be welcome.

When Sophia and Agnes Weston went on board the *Katori*, the latter was presented with a Japanese booklet which she was told was a translation of one of her own little books, *Underneath the Searchlight*. This told of the establishment and the running of the first Sailors' Rest at Devonport. The book had come into the hands of members of the Japanese Government who had ordered its translation, and a copy of this had been issued to every officer and rating in the Japanese Navy. As there was a fine photograph of Agnes Weston on the front page of the book, the men quickly recognised her and thought of her naturally as 'Mother Weston'. From the reports of the men who had visited the Rest in 1902, and the information gleaned from *Underneath the Searchlight*, the Japanese authorities had, by 1906, opened six homes similar to the Rests. When Miss Weston took some of the Japanese seamen to see the famous ship H.M.S. *Victory*, then afloat in Portsmouth Harbour, she was very surprised to see the visitors prostrate themselves before the place where Nelson had fallen, mortally wounded. The British nation had always revered the Admiral, but never paid him such homage as this. It is remarkable how the name of Nelson permeates the tradition and legend of the British Navy, even in this modern technological age. As it has been said, his ships have passed away, but his spirit remains the same. Consider how often in naval parlance you hear, 'The Nelson touch' or 'turn a blind eye'. The standards he set are still those to which the cream of the Navy aspires. All nations with a naval tradition honoured him, even the French sailors took off their caps when they passed the *Victory*, although Nelson had been France's most formidable enemy in the days of the Napoleonic Wars. He was unique for, although practically every fighting country had produced brilliant military leaders and outstandingly courageous admirals, there was only one Nelson.

Agnes Weston was also unique in her way, a peaceful way, although with her innate modesty she never considered herself out of the ordinary.

When the Japanese ships sailed for home, the men sent presents of embroidery to those who had served them so kindly at the Royal Sailors' Rest.

Agnes Weston was invited by the Japanese authorities several times to be their guest in Japan, for having started their Rests for the seamen they begged her to go and give them further advice. Much as she would have enjoyed such a task, Agnes felt that she could not spare the time; she did, however, let them have all the information she possibly could, and for this they seemed to be very grateful.

All international courtesies and amenities forge links in the chain which binds nations together, and certainly everything possible was offered by the Royal Sailors' Rest to the German seamen when they visited Plymouth in 1904. Agnes Weston told Admiral Sir Edward Seymour that she would like to share in the welcome of the German navy, and as an act of national hospitality, the members of the Rest would like the Germans to be their guests while they were in the Sound. The invitation met with the Admiral's approval and he promised to send the message to Admiral Von Koester, Commander in Chief of the German ships. Amidst the firing of salutes on both sides, the big warships moored, then among the signals hoisted in the fleet by Admiral Von Koester was one to the effect that Miss Weston cordially invited the men of the fleet to make the Royal Sailors' Rest their home while ashore. She wrote later, 'I can truly say the invitation was responded to; we were crowded out with bright, smiling Teuton blue-jackets, delighted with all they saw, and astonished even after the invitation at having nothing to pay!'

The Rest was resplendent with bunting outside and flew the German flag. Inside, there was so much to do that it was for Sophia Wintz just like the very first day the Rest opened—so many to feed, hundreds to look after and to talk to. Fortunately, Sophia's German was excellent, which Agnes found a great relief, for the little she had learnt when young had become very rusty. Music, singing, laughter, expressions of goodwill were heard everywhere, and the men were lost in admiration at the size of the Rest and all the arrangements made for the sailor's comfort. They were still more astonished when they realised the whole place was managed by two ladies. The visitors seized Agnes Weston's hand, and indulged in a series of *Hochs* which verily rent the roof. To take home with them the Germans were presented with literature from the Rest and copies of the Gospels in German. Nothing in this world is ever perfect, however, and on the last day of the visit, there happened something never known before or after—supplies of food ran out! Huge numbers had been anticipated, but even the Rest's staff had not expected the enormous rush of men which swept into the restaurant. Sophia explained the situation to the Germans and promised that in a short time everything would be normal; with the help of some of the British blue-jackets, an impromptu concert was organized in the big hall, while the staff set off to buy all the food they could get from the local stores, and the cooks prepared to cook the food as quickly as possible. The restaurant was soon replenished; the men replete and happy. No wonder hundreds of postcards of the Devonport Rest were sent back to Germany to show where the men were being given such a great welcome.

The hospitality shown to the German seamen made a great impression on them, so great in fact when they returned to the Fatherland, they were instrumental in getting similar Homes started in the big German ports.

A second visit of German seamen came in 1907 when the Kaiser and Kaiserin came to England to pay a brief visit to the British King and Queen. With the Imperial Yacht, the *Hohenzollern,* came the cruiser *Scharnhorst,* and the despatch boat *Sleipner.* During their short stay, the German seamen were entertained to a banquet which was attended by a large number of British sailors. After the meal there was entertainment for all. Agnes recalled that they bade the Germans adieu with regret and hoped to see them again. Just over seven years later, the First World War broke out and any thought of entertaining the German seamen for many years to come vanished. I wonder if her regrets were later tinged with bitterness, when she remembered how she had welcomed the boys as brothers to her British sons. Bitterness, however, was not one of her traits; she did what she believed was right, and more or less than that she could not do.

Agnes's connection with American seamen was a long and happy one. It began when the British and American ships were lying side by side at Yokohama and some copies of *Ashore and Afloat* as well as a Blue-back were given to the American sailors, and as the books passed from hand to hand, they were read eagerly and very much appreciated.

The American seamen asked if they could receive regular copies direct but Agnes Weston felt that she should get permission before despatching literature to other navies. She sent specimen copies to the Secretary of the Navy Board at Washington saying that if, in his opinion, the books were likely to do any good in the service, she would supply them with pleasure. A letter came back to thank her and suggested that she should send the copies in bulk to a London address, from which they would be distributed wherever American ships were stationed, and the Secretary added, 'Much I am sure to the pleasure of the men'.

Agnes made contact with the men towards the end of 1901, when she was asked to pay visits to two American warships and was quite overwhelmed by the kindness with which she was received. The two ships were the *Alliance* and the *Hartford;* the former was lying in Plymouth Sound, and the Captain sent a launch to take Agnes to the ship. As she went she must have thought back over all that had happened since her first journey to the *Impregnable,* when she had been so fearful in case the boys had not been interested in her speech, and how after the talk she had been so grateful to them for their wonderful response. Now she was neither a young woman nor timorous of her reception. When she arrived on the *Alliance* she was met by the Captain and then she talked to the men. She said that she hoped she had done some good, but at any rate she knew that she had made friends with them by the way they looked at her. When she left the ship, she was given three ringing cheers—cheers that rang true.

To go aboard the *Hartford* Agnes had to travel to London and then on to Gravesend. There was a fresh wind and the launch rolled heavily as she was taken to the *Hartford,* which had once been Admiral Farragut's flagship. Again, she was overwhelmed by her reception. 'I had such a welcome as Americans only can give; the band struck up, and the captain and officers seemed to vie with one another in cordiality', she wrote later.

She was conducted over the ship, and saw in the recreation rooms copies of *Ashore and Afloat* and also her monthly letters. These, she was told, were eagerly read from cover to cover. She addressed the men and, at the conclusion of her speech, the band struck up the National Anthem. After a cup of tea she returned to Devonport.

Agnes received many individual letters of thanks for the journals and was very touched by the genuine American gratitude.

She received a copy of Longfellow's poems from 'American sailor boys, with grateful thanks'. This beautifully bound book came from the lads of one of the United States training ships, whose chaplain wrote to tell Miss Weston how much they had all, officers and trainees alike, enjoyed reading *Ashore and Afloat* and the monthly letters.

She was always delighted to greet the Americans and said there must be a link between the White Ensign and the Stars and Stripes. While the American ships were at Kiel, she telegraphed Admiral Cotton saying that when they berthed at Portsmouth she would be pleased to welcome 400 men to a reception at the Royal Sailors' Rest.

The building was decorated for the occasion, the American flag being most conspicuous. As that fine body of men, 400 strong, marched up to be welcomed at the door by Miss Weston and Miss Wintz, the band was playing Sousa's march, *Stars and Stripes Forever*. A high time was had by the entire party, Americans and British: there were plenty of refreshments, then glee singing, recitations from the guests and the hosts, and to conclude a very memorable evening all joined hands for *Auld Lang Syne,* and as the guests marched off to rejoin their ships, the band played *Hail Columbia.*

'What wonderful friendship', wrote Agnes Weston in her diary that day.

During the Americans' stay in Portsmouth workers from the Rest visited the ships many times, making friends with the men, distributing Testaments and books. Demand for the Sailors' Testaments published by the Scripture Gift Mission was so great that the stock kept at the Rest was completely exhausted.

It was with real sorrow that Agnes Weston and all her helpers watched the American ships leave the harbour, and life returned to normal routine. It did not remain uneventful for long, for the arrival of the French fleet caused much excitement. Being such near neighbours, it was not uncommon for one or two French ships to be in our ports, and the red pom-pommed hats of the *matelots* usually caused no comment in the towns. The visit of the French Fleet in 1905, however, aroused much excitement, and even our own blue-jackets were excited over what they called the 'Tenty cordial'.

Portsmouthians, although used to the coming and going of foreign fleets, turned out *en masse* to greet the French ships, and the three-mile long Southsea front was thronged with waiting crowds. A few trails of smoke in the sky showed that the visitors were approaching, then the fighting-tops emerged, and lastly the ships themselves, moving majestically forward. Directly they were in British waters there was the thunder of guns as the two fleets saluted the French Republic and His Majesty the King of Great Britain. The ships took up their moorings at Cowes, where they stayed the night, and the next day got under way for their destination, Portsmouth. Because of the narrow harbour entrance the fleet came in single file, led by the flagship *Massena*. Again the people turned out in their thousands to greet the visitors, and the shores were crowded with cheering spectators. The massed bands crashed out the *Marseillaise*. The signal of welcome was given by the Royal Sailors' Rest, with the usual result. The *matelots* went there in their hundreds, and liked what they saw, and what they were offered, for the big hall had been turned into a café, with small flower decked tables and armchairs for relaxation, comfort indeed!

The hall was beautifully decorated with the *Tricolor* taking pride of place. Two large mottoes, one at each end of the hall, welcomed the visitors with *Bienvenue à la Flotte Francaise,* and *Vive L'Entente Cordiale.* Food was plentiful and altogether 34,765 rolls and cakes, 5,061 eggs, 2,771 bottles of soft drinks, 20 sides of bacon, and 120 joints of beef and mutton were consumed. After the meal there was entertainment from both hosts and visitors, including a display of swordmanship by Lieutenant and Mrs. Barrett. Following their initial visit to the Rest, the French sailors came back again and again; many had never been to England before and were amazed and delighted by the reception they received everywhere, and they were particularly touched by the warmth and friendliness of the people in the streets. The French sailors had always been led to believe by Continental cartoonists that the British were frigid and difficult people to get to know and that their women were plain to look at and icy if approached, but during this visit all these preconceived ideas were rapidly shattered.

Agnes Weston recalled that the Sunday was the happiest day of their visit. A religious service was announced for the afternoon, and anyone interested was invited. She did not expect 600 visitors to crowd in. The assembled men sang hymns in French and English simultaneously. 'It was beautiful', she said afterwards. The British sailors sang sacred solos and choruses. Then Agnes Weston spoke to them, saying that she spoke from the heart and hoped her words went to theirs.

The *Daily Mail* remarked about the visit, 'The French and the British paraded the streets arm-in-arm like sworn brothers. If their gait was not always steady you must put it down to hospitality, which the occasion excused. Proof of this might be found at the Sailors' Rests, where Miss Weston is the good angel who shelters those who have succumbed to the temptation of the moment'.

Again Miss Weston's workers were permitted to give souvenir books from the Royal Sailors' Rest, and 15,000 were given to the men who pressed for them and said that when they had read them they would send them home to their wives and mothers.

During this visit both nationalities had perhaps come to understand each other a little better; both certainly enjoyed the visit, and Agnes wrote, 'We did thank God that we had been able to take our small part in furthering *l'entente cordiale*'.

The interest in the Russian Navy went back for many years. Without British help the increase of Russian Naval power in the 18th century would have been much slower than it was, for it was British officers and leadership, British technicians and expertise, plus British goodwill which helped to found the Russian Navy under Peter I, preserve it under Anne and Elizabeth, then expand it under Catherine II. There were many British men teaching the 'know-how' in Russian ships, and many Russian seamen learning the 'know-how' in British ships.

Czar Peter came to England for a short stay in 1698 to study our methods of shipbuilding, and for his visit he rented Sayes Court at Deptford, which belonged to the great arboriculturist, John Evelyn.

Until the First World War, however, there were few visits from Russian Ships to our ports, so when in 1909 a fleet arrived, the sailors were warmly welcomed and 500 were invited to the Royal Sailors' Rest. Sophia Wintz organised the reception. She had the hall beautifully decorated and around the platform was banked a huge mass of flowers, which made a glorious splash of colour. The Marine Band played during the meal, and the caterers at the Rest gave of their very best. The meal was served as soon as the visitors arrived. A Russian officer acted as interpreter. No doubt the Rest staff could have made themselves understood, for they must have been used to speaking sign language with so many foreigners coming and going—and a smile of friendship is easily interpreted and means the same the wide world over. After the meal there was entertainment which did not need language; the Royal Naval Cadet Corps gave an exhibition of physical culture, and from the Royal Marine Artillery displays of fencing and gymnastics. Then came a charming show of classical dancing by the pupils of a ballet school. There were many British blue-jackets at the hall to mix with the Russians, and if they could not hold long conversations, they all applauded the acts with much enthusiasm.

Later a signal was received from the Admiral of H.I.M.S. *Cesarevitch* asking if a deputation of men could be received at he Rest before the ships sailed. The *Portsmouth Evening News* takes up the story:

'The deputation—three fine stalwart specimens of the Czar's Slav subjects—were accompanied by an officer to present them and to act as an interpreter. This he did in a charming manner, bowing very low and kissing hands. He desired first to thank Miss Weston for receiving the representatives of the crews who had come at the instigation of the men of the fleet to convey the unanimous appreciation of all for the hospitable reception of over 500 of them in the beautiful hall at the Royal Sailors' Rest, and to ask her acceptance of a small gift as a lasting memento of the hearty friendship the occasion engendered. Then one of the trio, an electrician, presented, with profound salutation, a handsome silver gift vase inscribed with these words:—

In Memory of
The Kind Reception at the Royal
Sailors' Rest
from
THE GRATEFUL CREW OF
T.R.S. CESAREVITCH

The deputation was made very welcome and a complete tour of

the building was made, during which many questions were asked and detailed answers given on the management of such an organisation, for like all other visitors, the Russians were eager to know if such Rest homes could be planned for their sailors. The day after the deputation had been received, the fleet of the *Cesarevitch, Slava, Olag* and *Bogatyr,* steamed away, and Agnes felt sure as they went that many good wishes followed them, and she earnestly prayed that the 500 copies of the Russian Scriptures distributed among the fleet might be a help and a blessing to those who read them.

With the Coronation of George V multitudes of foreign sailors flocked to the Rests, but huge as the number then was, it was as nothing compared to those who found a resting place there during the First World War, when the allied navies came into the home ports for recommissioning or for repairs; then the sailors knew where to go to be 'really at home'. During the 1914-1918 War Miss Weston entertained for the first time parties of women workers, nurses and others who came from the Colonies and from the United States to help with the war effort. When a large contingent of American nurses went for tea at the Devonport Rest, where they had a concert after the meal with the girls entertaining their hostesses, Miss Weston, then nearing the end of her life, must have thought back over all the years of friendship with the Americans, and how she had not only the sons of the U.S.A., but now the daughters too, as her friends.

At that time she also met women from all over the world who had come to England because of the war, and among those she greatly enjoyed meeting was Mrs. Alan Nickols—Mother of the American Flying Force. The Mother of the British Navy and the Mother of the American Flying Force must have had a great deal in common, one just finishing her long life, the other just beginning her work.

Agnes once wrote,

> 'A slender thread of kindness will sometimes do good, and I have endeavoured personally, by means of the Sailors' Rest, to make all welcome. The warmth with which these little kindnesses have been received, and the pleasure that they seem to have given to officers and men, has been a great

cheer to me and my fellow-workers, and my blue-jacket friends have also backed me up loyally'.

X

MUCH HAS been written about the work Agnes Weston did, and of her many achievements, far less about the woman herself. In fact her own writings tell us more about the things she liked and disliked, her opinions and so on, than we learn from those who actually knew her for it seems she very rarely talked about herself. The women who worked in the Rests and met her daily, the ex-sailors who were very young when they knew her but still vividly remember her, all tell a similar story—how kind, good, thoughtful, tolerant and unselfish she was—and recount a hundred stories to illustrate their rhapsodies. They remember her as a pleasant-looking rather than a handsome woman, whose best feature was her kindly grey eyes which could so often sparkle with laughter. The very mention of her name causes their own eyes to light up and the words to pour forth. Everyone talks of her calm expression of kindness which dissolved any feeling of tension when someone wanted to unburden his or her troubles, adding 'No wonder the men called her Mother, although some in the earlier days must have been several years her senior, for she was to them the ideal mother'. They told her much, for she was a ready listener, but about herself she told them little in return.

She was a robust woman and rarely away from the Rests and their ramifications. By far her longest absence was when she was cycling along Western Parade, Southsea, and her bicycle wheel caught in the tramlines and she fell and broke her leg. In her rather breezy way she describes the accident: 'In a moment I was over and heard the bone in my left leg snap like a carrot!'

She was rushed to hospital in the very cab she had swerved to avoid and while she was being attended to, the pain was so excruciating the doctor, fearing that she would faint, ordered some brandy for her—but she asked for, and was given, hot milk instead. Agnes later wrote,

> 'I do not look upon the taking of alcohol as a sin when given as a medicine, but I thought of many men and women too, to whom it was a great temptation; they had, I knew, been helped by my example, and would be discouraged and thrown back if I took the brandy, perhaps not knowing the circumstances under which it was administered'.

It was a novel experience for her to be inactive for two months, for from November 1896 until January 1897 she was in Portsmouth Royal Hospital; then she was taken out in a wheel chair; by the spring she was on crutches, and when summer came was walking as well as ever. Even while in hospital she continued to write her monthly letters and journal articles, and kept in touch with the business of the Rests by talks with Sophia Wintz or her other staunch helper, Miss Brown, during the daily visits. Agnes said after she had recovered that things had worked out for the best for the doctors' verdict was that the compulsory rest would give her ten years longer to work. Normally, she would have been irritated by this inactivity for she often wrote that inertia and laziness were anathema to her and stressed that she never wanted to belong to that great society in the world called, 'The Do-Nothings' whose coat of arms was false humility, and whose everlasting watch-words were 'I can't'. Moses had belonged to the Society once, so had Gideon, so had Jeremiah, and many others, but they had to leave it. God soon showed them that while of themselves they could do nothing, in Him they could do all things.

Agnes' watchword was love, all her work was based simply on love for her fellow men, and she often said,

> 'There is One who has taught us that our duty is the duty of love, "By love serve"—and the evolvement of love, if we are Christians at all, must blossom out in our lives. I have found through my life's experience that while ways and methods change, and we trust improve as the years roll on, the root principle "love" never changes but abideth for ever'.

To do the huge task she set herself was never easy; many sophisticated people were reluctant to associate with her unless she gave up her eccentric life and conformed more to the habits of society, while many Christian people disapproved of her methods of conducting the work and wished it done their way; some desired her to stop all entertainments and recreation, to put away all games and hoist the piano out of the window. Others wished all religious work of every kind stopped for they considered it uncongenial and morose. Some people ran tilt against conducting the Sailors' Rests on temperance lines. Agnes wrote that she never presumed to think that her way of working was the only way, but as she looked back over her life she could say, with all humility, that she felt she had been led step by step by God, otherwise she could have done nothing. Once asked if she were to begin all over again would she start as she had done before, she answered, 'Very probably in this 20th century it would be the last way of beginning a work for God in the navy—the old order changeth yielding place to the new, but it was all very different then, and that is the way my work commenced'.

She was a woman of many gifts, with any one of which she might have made a satisfying career and led a full life, but not, I am sure, as happy as the one she chose. She was extremely versatile—a competent business woman, a brilliant speaker, an accomplished writer whose short stories were read with avid interest when they appeared monthly, and also a very fine musician.

During her long service with the Navy upwards of two million pounds were entrusted to her by a generous British public every penny of which was carefully noted and subjected to audit year after year, and published in reports so that the reception and direction of every gift could be traced back for years. It was not only the handling of large sums of money and their use for the right purpose, but also the handling of the workmen she engaged which required her personal supervision. When Agnes and Sophia began to direct the alterations of the Co-op in Fore Street, the builders, carpenters, and furnishers must have thought that the job would be an easy and lucrative one with only two women to deal with—how wrong these men were they were soon to find out!

It was fortunate that Agnes was such an excellent speaker, for she had to convince the people that the large sums of money she was asking for were really essential for the continuance of her work. Right from that very first time when she had spoken to the sailor lads on their training ship, she found it easy to hold the attention of her audience, and later wherever she spoke—at a drawing room meeting, in front of a special Commission in the House of Commons, or to a crowded Town Hall assembly—she could always carry the day with her intense sincerity.

In 1885 the Church Assembly met at Portsmouth and the Bishop of St. Albans, who had previously been a vicar in the Portsea area, invited Agnes Weston to speak about her work. She was the first woman to be so honoured, and afterwards said that she didn't know if it was curiosity or what it was, but she had secured an audience quite out of proportion to her merits. The hall was crowded with clergy and others, and they seemed much interested in the account that she was able to give them. In 1901 she was asked to address the Church Assembly at Brighton; on this occasion the Bishop of Chichester was in the Chair, and Agnes was able to give her listeners a full account of her work with the blue-jackets. The people assembled listened with rapt interest. She begged the clergymen present to inform her when boys from their parishes were going into naval training, so that when they arrived at the ports, the mission workers could welcome them and give them full details of all the activities going on at the Rests.

Agnes was asked by Lady Henry Somerset if she would give a series of lectures to boost the Women's Temperance Association. After she had given the talks she declared her hope that she had given as much good to the meetings as she had received from them. Subsequently, she was invited to Duxhurst to visit the farm colony started there by the League's President, for the reclamation of inebriate women. The plan seemed so sensible and well thought out, Agnes could not think why someone had not thought of it before; it seemed so much better to give people a fresh start than to shut them away in prisons or in homes, and ostracise them from normal society. Later it gave Agnes much satisfaction to see how this plan was copied not only in this country but also abroad.

When the Duxhurst village was being built, Agnes interested some of the members of the Naval Temperance Society in the scheme, and they decided to raise the sum of money necessary to build one cottage. Agnes was the first to give a generous contribution, and others followed until there was not only sufficient to build the cottage but to furnish it also. H.R.H. the Duchess of Teck laid the foundation stone, and two representatives, a blue-jacket and a marine, were able to place a cheque and a purse of money on the stone to cover the entire cost.

One thing which gave Agnes Weston much satisfaction was to talk to the sailors, and the following incident shows how much they hung on her words. In the hall at the Portsmouth Rest she was once illustrating a point by telling the story of Pompey the Great, and when she described with virtuous anger how, after the Battle of Pharasalia, he was treacherously murdered, one of the sailors, moved by compassion, cried out 'Poor old Pompey', and this was echoed around the hall. A few days later some of the men were at Fratton Park watching a football match when the goal keeper fell headlong in the mud, trying unsuccessfully to stop the ball. One of the sailors shouted 'Poor old Pompey!' It appealed to the crowd who took up the call, and from then on it became the great port's nickname.

In 1916 a controversy arose among the prelates and churchmen as to whether women should be permitted to preach in Church, provided they addressed only women and children and that their lay female feet did not desecrate either pulpit or chancel steps. Agnes thought the whole discussion most amusing, for she had preached to men for forty years, and they would listen to their Mother Weston, whereas they would turn a deaf ear to the ordained clergy. 'But there', she said, 'you cannot expect them to cut the ground from underneath their feet, it isn't human nature, and after all's said and done even Bishops are human!'

Writing gave her great satisfaction, and of course her work had begun with letter writing. She used to say that it was just like talking to the men, and certainly it could not have been a labour, for while she was living at Lansdown she would retire to her room on a wet day and write forty letters. Her short stories were in great demand, and as soon as they were published more were eagerly sought, but as her work with the blue-jackets developed, her time for writing was limited. She wrote, and had printed, some very effective tracts on the need for temperance, and this theme she carried on in the official journal *Ashore and Afloat*. She soon devoted all her writing time to this magazine, which became very popular. From the first copy, Agnes was the chief contributor, but it was edited by Sophia Wintz. Its circulation grew until at the time of the First World War over half a million copies were being distributed half way around the world each month. It was not only service personnel who enjoyed it: the journal was read by policemen, postmen, railwaymen, young lads and old men, and all delighted in it. A writer from Canada told Sophia that *Ashore and Afloat* was eagerly sought in the backwoods, and she had letters begging for copies from as far afield as South America and Australia; while the Navy men read it from 'heel to truck', from the first page to the advertisement sheet. Sophia Wintz received many testimonials from her naval readers, and among them came the following, 'I am never at a loss for a piece or a song for the Temperance Meeting, that is if I have your paper with me, wherever it goes it sounds a clear note of warning, counsel and help'.

When King Edward VII visited the Rest at Devonport, he was so absorbed in the copy shown to him that he took it away with him and asked that further copies should be sent to him as they were issued.

Much of the tenor of Agnes's thoughts is revealed in her writings. The quality in men she wrote about often was physical courage, especially if laced with daring. Of sailors in general she wrote: 'No matter how hard the fight, they will dare all, our fellows are so courageous'. Time and time again in her journals she recounted deeds of courage in great detail, continuing the story month after month if it had particularly captured her imagination. Dealing as she did with the Royal Navy, whose service was active even in peacetime, she always had some heroic incident to report. During the First World War there were many acts of individual bravery for her to write about, and seldom a month passed without at least one or two paragraphs in *Ashore and Afloat* telling of some act of courage and heroism. Perhaps none stirred her admiration more than the bravery of the men of the *Broke*, with her daring Captain Evans and many heroes. It is evident that as she wrote her inspired article on the action, Agnes lived the men's heroic deeds over again with them. What greater courage could there be, she asked, than that of Able Seaman W.G.

Knowles, the *Broke's* heroic helmsman who was hit four times by shell fragments, but remained at his wheel throughout the action, and then fainted? She chuckled at the audacity of a stoker who was a day late reporting to the sick-bay although he still had a piece of shrapnel in his head, but gave the ingenuous excuse, 'I was too busy to come along, Sir', he explained to the surgeon, 'along of cleaning up all the rubbish on the stokers' mess deck'.

For women she wanted much, especially the vote, but she was not in favour of the violent methods of the Suffragette movement to obtain it. She knew they should have equal opportunities for learning, and thought that all education should be much wider than it was and include, amongst other things, swimming for everyone.

After 1914, when women took up so many unusual jobs in order to release men for the Services, she was inordinately proud of them and in one journal in 1916, wrote with pride:

> 'I am sure we do not yet fully realise what we owe to the part women have played in the war. Great, wise, and eminent men entrusted with Governmental powers, declared early in the war, in private and in public, that the nation was marching to ruin because it was being denuded of workers. What would become of our trade, we were asked. What of our exports? What of the means to finance our Allies? Would we, to quote one pretty phrase that sticks in my memory, "burst up the whole show", by drafting into the Army and out of production, indispensable, irreplaceable, irretrievable men? Little they recked, these pessimists, of what Woman could do. And it is not merely that women are serving as makeshifts or stop-gaps. In the great majority of cases the evidence shows they are doing their new job as well as men. Let me give you two very diverse illustrations of this important fact.
>
> Take the Army cooks as an illustration. On the outbreak of hostilities, to minimize the waste and to serve the food in a more palatable form, women cooks have been brought into service. Many of the women responded to the call, and the experiment has proved so successful that it is considered probable that women cooks will be retained after the war is ended.
>
> Thousands of women have registered as workers on the

land. If this wonderful spirit is sustained and I feel sure it will be, provided the farmers show patience towards new, inexperienced workers until they gain proficiency, and reward all by openly welcoming this revival of women and work in agriculture, then another great employment difficulty will have been solved'.

Proud as she was of the women workers, she wrote from the heart pleading with mothers of young families not to go out and leave their children. Be home when they get home she said, let them find the mother, the anchor of their lives, there for no one could possibly take her place. For many years Agnes published a page under the nom-de-plume of 'Aunt Susan', and Aunt Susan gave women, and occasionally men, very good advice, and helped them with their individual troubles. This must have been one of the first of the 'let me help you' pages, and it proved so popular that after Agnes Weston's death, Sophia Wintz continued it under the name of 'Aunt Mary'.

Miss Weston wrote with feeling on the brotherhood of man, and gave much publicity to anything which would illustrate our Saviour's words, 'Love thy enemy'. In the Boer War, after the battles when the wounded were taken to hospitals and cared for by either Boer or British medical teams, the men soon learned to fraternise, and she relates how a Boer soldier wanted a cigarette and immediately a wounded Tommy lit two and put one in the Boer's mouth and smoked one himself. Then the man who so recently had been his enemy burst into tears of remorse, reflecting no doubt on the futility of war. This was not, however, the general feeling for very many years, but it was not until after the First World War that men began to wonder why they should destroy one another for no real purpose. In 1916, when H.M.A.S. *Sydney* sank the *Emden* after the German ship had sunk over £2,000,000 of valuable shipping, mostly merchant ships, and the crew of the *Sydney* were besides themselves with elation, their Captain called the whole crew together on that eventful evening to thank God who alone had given them victory over the enemy and to ask for His love and mercy on all the widows and orphans that had resulted from the day's action. He went on to stress they were earnestly needed for the German widows and children in their hour of need.

Agnes believed strongly that any human being, whatever sex,

colour or creed, should be able to retain his, or her, dignity, and that all should be treated with a commonsense of fairness and judgement. The following paragraph appeared in an edition of *Ashore and Afloat* at the beginning of the 20th century:

'It has become commonplace to speak of equal rights for the white races in South Africa and elsewhere. Now, the first points of the Convention of 1881 were:— Better treatment of the Natives and equal rights for the white races. Those were righteous claims. Is it an advance or a retrogression that now we only hear of equality of the white races? Have the native races no rights? Will the Judge of all the earth have nothing to say about the rights of His coloured subjects in the settlement of South Africa?

We believe that the British Empire is the most free upon the earth and that it governs more fairly than any other nation those under its dominion. But there remains very much to be desired even in its treatment of the native races over which it has asserted and established its predominance.

A German merchant in Cape Town said, "We want no other than British rule in this colony, where Great Britain rules she treats the people alike all round; and what can we want more than that?" Yet in Durban the post-office has two entrances—one for whites and another for coloureds. Any loafer, be he white, may use the former, but a native, however well conducted, an Asiatic, however, cultured, though he might be an Indian Rajah, is condemned to use the other. Equality is one thing, equal rights another. The franchise is a responsibility which, by universal consent, must not be accorded without qualification—minority of age, mental incapacity, misconduct are universal disqualifications. It is right to withhold the suffrage from unqualified individuals of native races as of others. But it is not just to withhold any right from man because he is black or yellow, creole or mulatto, which would be accorded to him if he were white.'

She felt deeply also on affairs of injustice nearer home, but of the many she wrote about and sympathised with, none stirred her to such passion as the Dreyfus case. Month by month she reported on this, and when Dreyfus was imprisoned in the Sante and said,

'False friends are worse than enemies', in her monthly letter Agnes took this as her theme and begged her readers to consider his words. The trial certainly created a furore in Britain, and there were many angry demonstrations demanding his re-trial. Meetings were called, but the excitement was so great they invariably ended in chaos.

Agnes's writings were not all aimed at teaching or protests. Sometimes she wrote just for pleasure, and one of the topics she liked to talk over with her readers was cricket. It was a game she greatly admired, and very often she would insert items of news about well-known cricketers. She was quite sure that her women readers would be interested in these too, for, as she told them, the great W.G. Grace, was taught to play by his mother, and John Willes, another great cricketer of the time, who introduced round arm bowling, caught the trick from his sister. After a severe illness he sought to regain strength by getting his sister to bowl whilst he batted. He found her bowling very effective, and, noting that in delivering the ball she turned her hand over it, he decided to adopt the method himself.

Music she always enjoyed, whether she was accompanying on the organ the hymn-singing in one of the great halls at the Rest or listening to some very special performance. The listening varied— from judging singing competitions which she organised for the sailors' wives, among whom were discovered some very good singers who entered in national festivals, to being enthralled by the performances of world-famous musicians. Great artistes would feel honoured to give a performance for the sailors, and on Sunday afternoons the blue-jackets would throng into the halls at the Rests to listen to performers who were the very top of their profession. One such afternoon Clara Butt, accompanied by her husband, came to the Portsmouth Rest. She told her audience before the performance began, how pleased she and her husband were to be there to be able to show their appreciation of Miss Weston for all the great work that she did. At the close of that memorable concert came Clara Butt's superb rendering of *Home Sweet Home* and Agnes noted there was scarcely a dry eye in the whole assembly.

XI

IT HAS been said that had Agnes Weston been a man she would probably have scintillated like a rainbow with ribbons and medals but, as it was, not until within a few months of her death and after nearly half a century of service, did she receive the honour which gave her public recognition. For even when the custom which, with rare exceptions, excluded women from honours was broken down because of their service in the First World War, Miss Weston was not awarded the G.B.E. until the Birthday Honours of 1918, long after many who, according to public opinion, had been honoured for far less important work. But Agnes was a modest woman and never sought recognition or reward. The sailors said the G.B.E. stood for 'God bless 'er', and they rejoiced to the last man because she had received no less than her just reward. She was never personally presented with the decoration as she died before the investiture; the insignia was sent to her sister, who immediately forwarded it to the Royal Sailors' Rest at Devonport because, as Emily said, 'This belongs to everyone at the Rest, and I know Agnes would want it to stay there'.

Although her G.B.E. was given very late in her life, Agnes was accorded much honour during her life, which doubtless gave her great pleasure, for even the most dedicated of Christian workers must feel the pleasure of being appreciated sometimes. Agnes had so many incidents of spontaneous gratitude, to look back on such as when a woman took her hand and said, 'How can I ever thank you enough? I have had seven sons in the Royal Navy and I have

Chapter XI

never had any worry over them because they have been under your influence at the Rests. You have given them not only comfort, but you led them to a Christian life. God bless you, Miss Weston, and thank you'. She had the trust and affection of not hundreds but thousands of men, and this above all else, she wanted. But it always seems very sad that great reformers, authors, poets, painters, who are almost deified after death, while alive are totally ignored, for however immersed these people might have been in their work, they would have found some recognition gratifying, especially as knocks from critics are always so generously given.

In the last half of the 19th century the British Royal Family were the focal point of attention. Wherever they went, whatever they wore, whatever they did, made headlines. The majority of the people in this country lived such drab lives that they looked upon those who lived at Court as people in a different world. Agnes Weston was among the millions of staunch supporters of the Royal Family, but it was many years before she was actually invited to meet Queen Victoria, for it is said—with how much truth it is difficult to say—that the Queen had an ingrained prejudice against one of her own sex taking up work of a public character, and that a woman like Agnes should accomplish so great a service for the Navy without the help of a husband did not recommend her to Royal favour. Eventually, however, when they did meet, the Queen's admiration for Miss Weston and for her work was very clear.

In the course of their vocation both Miss Weston and Miss Wintz met many members of the Royal Family, but it was not until 1887 that they had their first Royal visitor, when the Crown Princess of Germany, the eldest daughter of Queen Victoria, asked if she might pay her respects to the ladies who ran the Rests. Agnes and Sophia, quite unused to Court etiquette, were a little apprehensive but they need not have been, for the charm and naturalness of the Princess put everyone at ease. Sophia acted as hostess, and Agnes showed their visitor round the establishment and explained the running of the huge home. It was clear at this first meeting that the Royal visitor was in instant rapport with Agnes Weston, and before she left, the Crown Princess said that if circumstances had been different she would have liked to have joined forces with her and worked for the good of the men. Soon after this visit a cheque was received for 30 guineas to endow a cabin, which was to be named after the Crown Princess's son, Prince Henry.

By all accounts the Crown Princess was a very beautiful woman who had inherited the sensitivity and intelligence of her father and the kindliness of her mother—a precious combination. It was a pity that Agnes never knew Prince Albert: they would have had so much in common and he would have esteemed her intelligence very highly and given her work every possible encouragement.

Many years later, in 1898, the Royal Princess paid her second visit to the Portsmouth Rest; she was then the Empress of Germany. The Diamond Jubilee Block had just been completed and it was suggested that the Empress Frederick should be invited to open it. There had been great excitement all over the country at both the Golden and Diamond Jubilees, and to no one more so than one of the blue-jackets at the Rest who got drunk on both occasions and said he would be at all the other Jubilees, whatever precious stones they were named after.

The day of the opening was bitterly cold, but the Empress and her suite arrived exactly on time and were met with rousing cheers from the sailors and the townspeople, for she was always a popular visitor to Portsmouth, and had been well known there as Britain's Princess Royal.

After her reception the Empress was led on to the platform in the big hall—it was packed with an audience combining local dignitaries and naval ratings and their wives and families. The Empress told the assembly how she had followed the growth of the Royal Sailors' Rests, and that Miss Weston's work had always been very dear to her heart. After Agnes had presented a short progress report, the Royal visitor was handed a silver key with which to undo the door of the Diamond Jubilee Block. The party then began to tour the new building but, as they reached the upper floor, the Empress asked Agnes Weston if the two of them could continue together without the rest of the party. When safely inside a cabin the Empress wept unrestrainedly and unburdened her troubles to Miss Weston, as one might have done to a sister, then she controlled her feelings again, and they continued their tour. It was the last visit of the Empress to the Rests, for she died in 1901. She had had so much trouble to bear and it must have been very difficult for her to find someone as sympathetic as Miss Weston to whom she could talk without fear of her confidence being repeated.

Agnes became acquainted with the Duke of Edinburgh, later the Duke of Saxe Coburg and Gotha, when they worked together after the sinking of the *Serpent,* and it is possible that through his influence she was invited to exhibit an example of her work in the grounds of the Chelsea Hospital in London at the Royal Naval Exhibition in 1892. She was offered a strategically good position for her display and readily accepted. A mock-up of a full-sized cabin was erected and fitted out exactly like those in the Rests. Outside was a figure of a blue-jacket holding a telescope, standing by a flagstaff. The whole scene was made as realistic as possible. The Rests' organisation also undertook to provide accommodation for the sailors on duty at the Exhibition. This took the form of a bungalow, a sort of Sailors' Rest with a difference. It was very inviting, surrounded by a small garden ablaze with scarlet geraniums and yellow calceolarias. The interior comprised a restaurant, a reading room and, next to it, a writing room, and behind these a mess-room where those on duty could dine and talk. A small room was set aside as a quiet room for Bible study or prayer. The cook's galley and usual offices completed this very attractive building, and right round the bungalow was a very wide verandah. The men used to sit out there and smoke and play on their banjos and mandolins. One can imagine they were never without an admiring audience. Naturally the authorities were more than satisfied; what better advertisement could there be for naval comfort and, seeing the men enjoying themselves so much, what better enticement for recruitment? Not the least appreciative was the Duke of Edinburgh, and when the Prince and Princess of Wales went to the Exhibition, he presented Agnes Weston and her staff to them. Princess Alexandra charmed everyone with her graciousness and beauty, and from the time of that meeting she became very concerned with the work and, as with so many good causes, a most generous contributor.

The Naval Exhibition ran for 151 days, during which time it attracted 2,351,683 visitors and made a profit of £48,000 which was devoted to the widows and orphans of naval men.

Subsequently, and no doubt through the influence of the Duke, the Queen let it be known that she was willing to bestow the prefix 'Royal' upon the Sailors' Rests. This was confirmed by Royal Warrant, proclaiming that it was a fitting title for Royal work. It must have given Miss Weston and all those who worked with her a satisfying sense of 'at last we are established'. Even that industrious little team would have not been too busy to sit down and reflect, 'Now we've a Royal Warrant for the Homes of men who, half a century earlier were a mere rabble, wanted by few; we've come a long way'. One can easily imagine Miss Weston's caustic postscript too, 'Yes, and we've still a long way to go'.

Queen Victoria also ordered that, when her son's command expired, a cabin should be endowed by her. This caused much excitement among the men for she was a national figure and was much loved. She took a personal interest in the fittings of the cabin and said that a portrait of herself should hang in it. Miss Weston, with her usual tact, called together a committee of sailors to select a suitable likeness. Opinions were many, the picture of the Queen in her widow's cap and writing a letter was declared too sad, others not as the Queen really looked; it seemed as if there could be no agreement until quite suddenly someone suggested the regal picture of Victoria in crown and carrying her sceptre. Everyone agreed that this was an excellent choice and so for many years this Royal portrait hung in the cabin.

In 1898 Agnes received a summons to go to Windsor to talk over with Her Majesty the work being done for the sailors. Agnes was certain that the Queen had been encouraged to issue this invitation through the reports given by H.R.H. the Duke of Edinburgh and the Empress Frederick. On the way to the Deanery at Windsor where she was to stay, she wondered what she could say to keep the Queen interested for the fifteen-minute interview—suppose the Queen found the stories of the naval men and their wives not to her liking, supposing the whole meeting fell flat? Agnes went over time and time again the things she wanted to say to the Queen, and there is no doubt that she was more than a little apprehensive about the whole affair. Then she was told by her hostess that she had better prepare to kiss the Royal hand. She practised and practised for hours on end, and time and time again the curtsey and the withdrawing walk; such formal court presentations for the select few have finished, but then the ordeal was regarded with enormous solemnity.

When she reached the Castle Agnes was taken through a sequence of rooms and eventually was left alone in a huge chamber, magnificently furnished, banked with flowers and rich with pictures and statuary.

When the Queen arrived, so small, so gracious, all Agnes's fears faded, as did her well rehearsed anecdotes, for they talked naturally as two people must who have a common interest; Agnes found that her Queen wanted to know all that she could be told about the Rests and the men in them. It was after forty minutes, not the usual fifteen, that Agnes withdrew, but not before she had kissed the Queen's hand!

At Windsor the ways and sayings of the Queen were naturally the chief topic of conversation, and one that Agnes heard during her stay she felt bound to put in her next edition of *Ashore and Afloat*—it was that the Queen often said, 'Let me never hear the word "trouble", only tell me how the thing is to be done rightly, and I will do it if I can'.

The crowning pleasure to this visit came after her return to the Rest when Agnes received, by special messenger, a signed portrait of the Queen. She knew then she had been a welcome visitor.

The Queen had told Agnes that she would have liked to receive her at Osborne, and eventually Agnes did go to Osborne, but not to be entertained by Victoria. For it was in 1901 that she went, at the invitation of Queen Alexandra to pay her last respects to her beloved Victoria, the great Queen and Empress, as she lay in her small coffin enjewelled only by the Jubilee Crown.

Everyone in Britain mourned the death, and when the bier was taken from the Isle of Wight to the mainland thousands of people turned out to say their last good-byes. Every woman found something black and suitable for such an occasion, while every man wore a black crepe arm band. Men as well as women wept unashamedly in the streets. The funeral cortège was very impressive, the big ships guarded the Solent, while the little *Alberta,* accompanied by yachts, bore the coffin. How many times I have heard tell how, when the *Alberta* was half way across the harbour the clouds parted, as in Biblical times, and a ray of sunshine played on the coffin. For some this was a prophetic sign, for others a suitable parting, but it heightened the drama of the day. Later in the afternoon the Navy played a distinguished rôle for, as the horses which were pulling the funeral carriage became restive, the sailors untethered the animals and took the dray-ropes and hauled the coffin to St. George's, that most beautiful of chapels at Windsor.

This was a day when not only a Queen died, but a whole phase of English life ended and a new era of life began.

1901 was a busy year for Miss Weston and feeling in need of rest, she bought a small house at Grayshott, near Hindhead in Surrey. According to the writer, Thomas Wright, Hindhead was then called 'the English Switzerland', such was its beauty, 800 feet above sea-level, forested with pines and surrounded by miles of purple-heathered common. Previously, this stretch of country had had a bad reputation; coach robberies had been so frequent that an extra mounted guard had been attached to the stage-coach at Godalming to see the passengers safely through the hilly country. One hill at Hindhead is still called Gibbet Hill, although the gibbet blew down in a violent storm in 1790. It had been erected to hang three men who had murdered a sailor for the little money and few possessions he had. They were arrested the day after the crime and taken to Kingston to be tried. They were gibbeted on 7 April 1787, perhaps on this spot as a warning to others! The Sailor's Stone now stands in Thursley Churchyard, near Hindhead, depicting in stone the three ruffians murdering the unfortunate sailor, while the lower part of the stone bears the words:

> 'When pitying eyes to see my Grave shall come,
> And with a generous tear bedew my Tomb;
> Here shall they read my melancholy fate.
> With Murder and Barbarity complete.
> In perfect Health, and of the Flower of Age,
> I fell a Victim to three Ruffians' Rage
> On bended Knees I mercy strove t'obtain,
> Their Thirst of Blood made all entreaties Vain.
> No dear Relations or still dearer friend
> Weeps my hard lot or miserable End.
> Yet o'er my sad remains (my name unknown)
> A generous public have inscribed this Stone.'

When Nicholas Nickleby was walking with Smirke to Portsmouth

XVI JACK'S TREASURES

XV SAYING GOOD-BYE TO 'GRANNY'

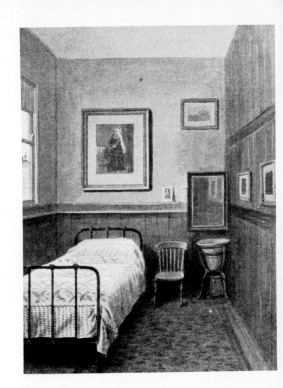

XVII A 'CABIN',
presented by Queen Victoria

XVIII OFF DUTY ON H.M.S. *BONAVENTURE*

XIX ROYAL SAILORS' REST, DEVONPORT, after the blitz, 22 April 1941

XX ROYAL SAILORS' REST, PORTSMOUTH, after the blitz, 10 January 1941

XXI CLEARING THE SITE OF THE ROYAL SAILORS' REST, PORTSMOUTH

we read of Hindhead through Dicken's eyes.
"They walked to the rim of the Devil's Punch Bowl, and Smirke listened with greedy interest as Nicholas read the inscription upon the stone which reared up on that wild spot, tells of a foul and treacherous murder committed there by night."

It seems that Agnes never, so far is known, made reference to the works of Dickens, yet they had so much in common, being both good story tellers, both very much concerned with underprivileged members of society. In her writings, in order to bring home a point, Agnes often quoted from classical writers when an example from a novel by Dickens would have been more apt. In one very odd way, however, their names were joined. Once there was a menagerie visiting Portsmouth, and the lioness gave birth to two cubs. The manager requested the Mayor of Portsmouth to go along and name the new arrivals. The ceremony was attended by crowds of townspeople, and the names voted by common consent were, 'Charles Dickens' who was born in Commercial Road, Portsmouth, and 'Agnes Weston' because she had done so much for the 'lions of the sea'.

To return to Hindhead, by 1901 all dangers had passed and most people, including Agnes and her friends, were delighted by the beauties of the district—one dissentient voice, however, was that of William Cobbett, who declared it the most villainous spot that God ever made, adding that our ancestors seem to have ascribed its formation to another power, for the most celebrated beauty spot there is still called the Devil's Punch Bowl. Not far from Ensleigh at Grayshott, the house Agnes named after her Bath home, is Grayshott Hall, a manor house which was once owned by Tennyson and where he wrote some of his most admired poems.

While Ensleigh was being altered to suit its owner's taste, Agnes and her friends camped out on the heath. They found life idyllic, revelling in their freedom among beautiful surroundings and, moreover, Grayshott was only forty miles from Portsmouth, with an excellent train service running from Haslemere to the port.

Their retreat was short-lived, for pressure of work made it difficult for Agnes and Sophia to be long absent from the Rests, and we read in *Ashore and Afloat,* a touching little notice: 'To let furnished Ensleigh at Grayshott, Hindhead, Surrey, to someone who would benefit from it, or if preferred the house could be sold, very reasonably'. It was a typical Westonian observation: nowadays, everyone thinks of making an enormous profit from property—'Aggie,' as the blue-jackets affectionately called her, thought that property should profit someone else.

It was at Grayshott during that summer of 1901 that Agnes Weston received the news that an honorary degree, a Doctorate of Law from the University of Glasgow, was to be bestowed upon her. As ever she saw this as an honour for all the team, given to her to be shared. She was very excited, for the University, founded in about 1450, had never before conferred an honorary degree on a woman. Now four women had been selected for the honour. The first was Mrs. Campbell of Tullichewan Castle in the Lowlands near Loch Lomond, who had devoted a great deal of her time to the higher education of women, a cause in 1901 much frowned upon by the majority of people, who considered that even elementary schooling for girls was a complete waste of public money. The second lady was Miss Davies, the founder of Girton College, Cambridge who had pioneered its development—not an easy task, for Cambridge was then, and remained for many years to come, a male stronghold. Thirdly, Mrs. John Elder, who had given large donations to the Glasgow University was to receive her degree as a 'thank you' for her generosity; unfortunately she was too ill to be present at the ceremony. Lastly, there was Agnes Weston to be honoured for her philanthropy and her great social work.

Sophia Wintz went with her to Glasgow, and according to those who knew them both, although Sophia was the frailer of the two, it was she who looked after Agnes.

'Always saw she was wrapped up', said one of their helpers. 'You knew Miss Weston would be so busy she would forget to look after herself, then Miss Wintz would step in and take care of her', from another, 'She'd put a fur round her shoulders on a cold night or a scarf for her neck, real kind and thoughtful she was'. 'Real thoughtful', seems to be the general and loving opinion of Sophia Wintz. So we can be quite sure that she saw that they had all they needed for their trip to Glasgow. They stayed with Professor and Mrs. Cleland, who were old friends. For such a pioneer as Agnes Weston this must have been just the excitement she really enjoyed—she was making history, one of the first four

Chapter XI

women Honorary Doctors at Glasgow. What would be next, how far would women go in leading their country? All these questions and more must have gone through her head, for at this time no British woman had any hope of having the vote, and Agnes Weston realised that what she was doing was paving the way for the acceptance of women on a level of equal intelligence with men. There was a long way to go, of course, and many a male intransigence before women eventually received the recognition.

The three women met the men who were to receive degrees in the Assembly Hall at 10 o'clock. The gathering was a formidable body of celebrities included Lords and Bishops from England, Scotland and Wales, and professors from India, Europe and America. Such a body of savants impressed Agnes so much that she declared it was worth the journey to Scotland to see even such an assembly. Here again is an example of Agnes' endearing characteristic, modesty—it was not she who was important, but all the other people who had gathered who were so famous and clever.

Bute Hall was crowded to overflowing as the procession filed in, to the organ accompaniment. Lord Kelvin opened the ceremony with a fine speech, then the presentations began. The first to take the oath and to enrol their names were the Doctors of Divinity; each was then invested with a hood of his order. After a pause the Dean of Law, arrayed in his scarlet robes, addressed the Assembly and explained that the University was determined to think of women as being worthy of academic awards, and so, for the first time, was awarding them the University's highest honours.

It was a triumphant occasion for the women when the whole audience rose to their feet as one man to show their enthusiasm. Then, as if to mark the contrast, after the solemn ceremony the undergraduates started to cheer, and accompanied by the organ struck up with *For she's a jolly good fellow*. While the procession glided from the great doors the undergraduates massed in an excited group—they let the gentlemen pass in silence, but when the three women came the young men threw up their caps and cheered until the whole place seemed to vibrate under their enthusiasm.

After this there came a short period of relaxation; the two friends were invited to parties and dinners, where Agnes Weston received many congratulations. She said when she got home and after all the excitement had died down, 'I hope such appreciation may encourage workers in every field of Christian enterprise'.

Perhaps after such an honour as receiving the LL.D. the following tribute may seem to be an anti-climax, but it was bestowed with a good faith. In the 1914–1918 War some blue-jackets wrote home from the Dardanelles, 'She don't forget us, and we don't forget her. We've named a gun after her, the 'Agnes Weston', and don't she speak out. When she speaks there's not many can stand up against her!'

Agnes hoped that she would die in harness, and her wish was granted. She returned from a long spell in Portsmouth to the Devonport Rest in June 1918. She always felt at home in Plymouth, she often used to say how pleased she was that she had been called to start her work in the beautiful county of Devon, and in the town of Drake and Raleigh, and the last point in England of the Pilgrim Fathers, who were so brave as to seek freedom of worship in the New World.

Although she continued to do her daily work when she returned to Devonport, Agnes had no wish to appear in public or to go out of her rooms. On Tuesday 22 October 1918 she was working in her office-cum-sitting room until supper time and appeared to all her staff particularly bright and cheerful, in fact just her usual dear self. As she got ready to go to bed, she closed her books and said 'Thank God, another day's work done'.

Early the next morning she had a heart attack, and shortly afterwards passed away; before she died she was able to say to her friend, who was standing by her bed, 'Don't trouble about me, I'm all right'.

When Sophia Wintz took over the administration she found everything in such perfect order that it might have been planned. All letters had been answered, all bills paid, receipts filed, notes on questions in hand made in detail, and even the material for the Christmas publication of *Ashore and Afloat* was written, including 'Jottings from my Log'. These were the last words Mother Weston wrote to her sons:

'JOTTINGS FROM MY LOG–DECEMBER 1918
Dear Friend,
Another Christmas has come to us, and although sorrow

unmeasurable has come upon us during the past year, there is nothing to prevent the peace of God like the beautiful twilight of the lapland midnight, from filling our hearts with rest if we do not bar it out ...
[She then speaks of the first Christmas, and of the importance of making every child happy at Christmas and then, very unusually, she goes on to talk about herself]
... It is not given to us always to be well, and I am sorry to have to say that I have to take things very quietly in my Devonport quarters, and have been ordered to remain in my bed and sitting rooms, which are fortunately alongside one another, because the doctor tells me that I have been suffering from a tired heart, which must have rest. He tells me that if I do not do this I shall be quite unable to steer our big Sailors' Rests in the storm and stress of our present difficult days. This being so I have succumbed to the good advice and am at present in my room. The outlook is very pretty; I am on the first floor, the Admiral's garden is before, behind rolls the blue waters of the Tamar, making a harbour called the Hamoaze. The big ships come and go, torpedo destroyers flash up, and fussy little motor boats are always on the go. Behind, again, stretch the Cornish hills and the sunsets, which turn the water into golden roadways, are something to be seen.

I cannot be thankful enough that God enables me to do my work and so to keep the bridge surrounded by a splendid band of capable and true helpers. Miss Wintz is with me as full of energy as ever and, Portsmouth, with its band of tried workers, is holding the fort and doing the work well, and the winter there finds the campaign going with a full staff and full meetings. Several hopeful schemes that I had in view have had to be dropped, but God knows, and disappointments are always His appointments. ...
[She talks then of the joy it gives her to see the Air Force men using the Rests with other forces, and ends as usual].
      Believe me,
         Yours very sincerely,
           AGNES E. WESTON.'

It was found later that she had designed her memorial window to be in stained glass and portraying herself wearing her gown as a Doctor of Law. This window was later unveiled in Plymouth at a small but very touching service by the Bishop of Exeter.

Agnes Weston was buried with full naval honours; the first time such an honour had been accorded to a woman. In attendance were 2,000 officers and men, with them representatives from the R.A.F., the W.R.N.S., and naval personnel from the United States and Japanese navies who wished to show their respects. A short service was held in the Dockyard Church, and the Reverend Dr. Flynn gave the address which he based on the 20th verse of the first chapter of Phillippians—'According to my earnest expectation and my hope, that in nothing I shall be ashamed, but that with all boldness, as always, so now also Christ shall be magnified in my body, whether it be by life or by death'.

He said that he was an old naval chaplain who, for 30 years, had had the privilege of knowing Miss Weston, and told of her 45 years' strenuous labour to the glory of God and the good of the Service. Her work, he said, was written not only in bricks and mortar but in the lives that were blessed, in the homes that were made happy and bright and in the souls saved through her endeavours. Her work had gone on so long that the men almost thought it must go on for ever. He spoke of her great love, her philanthropy, her honesty and her wonderful power of attracting and attaching men and women to her, rich as well as poor. On that day, north, south, east, west, wherever the White Ensign fluttered, there was sorrow at sea, for every officer, man and boy who knew Agnes Weston knew they had lost in her a great friend.

The address ended with the words, 'The earth is poorer and heaven richer because "the Sailors' Friend" has passed away'.

The roads from the Dockyard Chapel to the Corporation Cemetery at Weston Mill were lined with thousands of men and women who wanted to say their last goodbyes. The coffin, covered by the Union Jack, was placed on a gun carriage; it bore three wreaths only. The hundreds of other floral tributes were carried by the blue-jackets. The procession was headed by the band of the Royal Marines who played the Chopin and other funeral marches, and at the grave the committal prayers were said by the Rev. Dr. Flynn. The escort having presented arms, the bugler sounded the Last Post, bringing to a close the impressive service.

Messages of sympathy poured in, from the King and Queen, from the Prince of Wales and from Queen Alexandra. The latter wrote: 'Miss Weston, whose untiring work for the navy will always be gratefully remembered by the sailors, to whom her whole life and energy were devoted'. Of all the tributes, I think the one which would have been nearest to Agnes's heart was that from her dear friend, Lord Charles Beresford:

> 'The whole Navy appreciated her untiring energy, her chivalrous and unselfish work in trying to benefit the men on the lower deck. I have lost an affectionate friend, but the good she has done will live after. I value and remember her as one of the finest and most admirable characters amongst women. It will be some slight consolation to you to know the universal respect and affection that is attached to the memory of Miss Weston.'

After that there can be nothing to add.

XII

AT THE end of October 1918, Sophia Wintz assumed the entire responsibilities of the management of The Royal Sailors' Rests with all the multitudinous activities this involved. In 1920 she too was honoured when King George V made her a Dame of the British Empire. This well-deserved recognition was warmly welcomed by her many friends, not least of whom were the hundreds of sailors' wives who met her regularly at the Rests.

She bore the loss of her friend with characteristic fortitude and asked only that she should live long enough to see a fitting memorial put up to Dame Agnes. This was to be a new block of some 200 cabins and a series of recreation rooms to be added to the Devonport Rest. The land for this additional wing had been purchased some time before Agnes' death and the plans had been prepared but since large building projects not directly connected with the prosecution of the war could not be entertained at that time the plans had had to be shelved. Sophia was determined that, at the end of hostilities, the new block should be built and should become a memorial worthy of a great woman. It took some time because materials were scarce in the early post-war years and the country was extremely unsettled; after much delay, the construction was finished in 1924; it made the Rest in Devonport the largest temperance home for service men in the world. As a personal memorial to her friend, Sophia had erected at the head of Agnes' grave, a figure beautifully carved in white marble standing on a base of rock in which is embedded an anchor.

Chapter XII

The years to come needed all Sophia's patience and ingenuity for they were indeed difficult years. War had exhausted the country, and the civilians who had been conscripted wanted only one thing, to be demobilised and get back to their families and their regular jobs. These years of demobilisation were succeeded by the drastic cutting down of the armed forces, when the Rests were comparatively quiet; the days of full to overflowing Rests were not to return for almost twenty years. Prices were rising rapidly, goods were in short supply, taxation was heavy, times were hard. Sophia stood back and took stock of the whole situation: one thing she knew she must not do was to get into debt. She wrote in *Ashore and Afloat:* 'Our great desire has always been to give the men the best of everything at the lowest possible prices, but now I am faced with the problem of getting sufficient money to carry on as before, so I am forced to raise the price of the cabins from 6d. to 1/- per night'. At the same time she introduced comfortably furnished bed-sitting rooms for those who wanted to be on their own and to make life more snug and self-contained for those wishing to stay for a longer period. These bed-sitting rooms proved so popular that in 1934 fifty more were provided.

One of the very last things Sophia did was to compile the 1927/28 Annual Report. It was so full and so interesting that one feels she must have realised it would be her last. It started with the theme of love and she wrote, 'What would the world be without love?' Then she told of the importance of a loving wife to a sailor who is often away from home for long periods. She traced the growth of the Rests, the changes that had taken place in the Navy. She praised the supreme leadership of Nelson and other great naval commanders and concluded by giving praise to her helper, Colonel Charles Weston, whom she knew would continue the good work after her death. Then came the detailed accounts for the year, among which was her own donation of £200.

During the last six months of her life Sophia Wintz was very frail. She bore her pain with accustomed fortitude and patience, but towards the end of 1928 it became obvious to her friends that her bodily powers were rapidly weakening, though the brain was as alert as ever. The end came peacefully in the early hours of a dark winter's morning on 16 January 1929.

Everything had been left in the most meticulous order and the Trustees on whom devolved the task of carrying on the administration of the Rests were able to take up the threads at once, with the steadfast and loyal co-operation of the staffs at Portsmouth and Devonport. In a letter opened by the trustees after her death, Sophia asked for only one thing, that the inscription 'We loved, we love, we shall love' should be engraved on the base of the headstone of her grave.

Immediately Admiral Sir Rudolf Bentinck, K.C.B., C. in C. Plymouth, learnt of Miss Wintz's death he ordered that she should be given a naval funeral, as Miss Weston had had before her. Tributes were many, and among these was one from *The Times;*

'She was a woman of great intellectual vigour and capacity and had an unaffected charming personality which endeared her to all associated with her. Like her coadjutor, Dame Sophia had the support and friendship of the King and Queen, and many other members of the Royal Family in her philanthropic undertakings'.

Colonel Weston's very simple and sincere appreciation was, 'One of the noblest women of her day and generation passed to her award'.

Early in 1929 the following appreciation appeared in *The Children's Newspaper:*

'Two quiet ladies and Jack

Everyone knows that women can do wonderful things today, but we often forget the wonderful things they did yesterday.

Nearly 60 years ago, for instance, two ladies quietly decided to look after the men of the Royal Navy. Perhaps someone said, "That's a man's job". "Then the men are doing it badly", the ladies may have answered. They said that when Jack is ashore it is a shame to tell him, "You can wander up and down the streets in the rain, or you can go to a public house".

The ladies said the streets were not good enough for tired sailors; something must be done—and they did it.'

Looking back over those long years of hard work and devotion to others, one cannot fail to be impressed by the way two women of totally different personalities blended into an ideal partnership.

Chapter XII

Agnes Weston was the instigator and Sophia Wintz, the continuer. Miss Weston had great gifts as a public speaker and as a writer; Miss Wintz was a very able administrator; both were first class business women. That the combination was irresistable is proved by the way in which they overcame the obstacles in their way, some of which were formidable.

It was gratifying to know that a Weston was to continue the administration; it had been suggested to Miss Wintz that she should change her name to Weston when she took over control after the death of Agnes but, although amused, she rejected the idea saying that her father had been very proud of the name Wintz and so was she. Charles Weston was a kindly, modest man who was quite overwhelmed at the thought of following two such forceful characters. He had had a varied career, having been commissioned in the Army before the war and served overseas, before spending a short but happy time in Canada as a school bursar. He became Sophia's assistant until her death when, at her request, he was appointed Hon. Treasurer and Hon. Manager. How unsure he was of his capabilities is illustrated by this letter he wrote when he commenced his new responsibilities:

'Dear Friends,

It is with a heavy heart and a most unaccustomed pen that the writer tries to pick up the threads dropped by her, whose hand had so long been on the tiller, on January 16th.

The Trustees are convinced that *Ashore and Afloat* is far too valuable a link with the men of the Service and our many other friends to be allowed to come to an end.

Shortcomings there will be and mistakes of inexperience must arise, and are pleaded and apologised for in advance. Dame Sophia was gifted in so many ways, and I fear that her natural flair for the written word will be found lacking in her successor ...'.

If Sophia's years of administration in the immediate post-war Britain had been difficult, they were nothing compared to the years when Charles Weston carried the work on through the Depression. But carry on he did and his helpers admired this gentle, kindly man who saw so much good in others yet was himself so self-effacing and diffident.

In 1937 he relinquished his responsibility to Mrs. Bernard

Currey, who held the post of Hon. Lady Superintendent and later, Trustee-in-Charge until 1958 when she was succeeded by Commander Savage. During her period of office she piloted the Rests through some stormy years.

Colonel Weston continued to edit *Ashore and Afloat* until his marriage in 1946. He died suddenly in Portsmouth on 19 January 1948, and was buried at Whitchurch Canonicorum, the lovely Dorset village in which he had lived for many years. He had so endeared himself to the villagers that they asked to shoulder his coffin to the small churchyard. As they lowered his bier they covered it with jasmine from his garden, and two feathers from Felix, his gander, which had been his constant companion for twenty-four years.

Within two years of Charles Weston's resignation the Second World War broke out. Instant conscription meant that once again the Rests were teeming with men, this time men from all three armed forces. The war was different from any that had been fought before; there was no jingoism, for this was no flag-waving affair but a war of total commitment. The British people accepted it almost philosophically, and strangely enough almost gladly, for the previous years of uncertainty had been very trying; the general view was a job had to be done—that of crushing Nazism—and the quicker it could be done the sooner life would return to normality. It was a naive view in the light of what actually happened.

The first year of the war, for this country, was comparatively quiet, but by mid-1940 every Britisher knew the force of modern weapons. Agnes would have been proud of the people whose courage will for ever be considered as the ultimate—the people of London during their ordeal in the raids; the superb courage of the Services throughout the whole war; the fleet of small ships at Dunkirk; the stamina of those who lived in the ports; in short, the whole British nation.

It was to be expected that when the Germans started to bomb this country, the ports would bear the brunt of the attack. Whether or not they were not too careful where they unloaded their bombs, from sheer frightfulness, incompetence, or because they were harried by the 'Few', in fact a large proportion of German bombs fell on the homes of the populace. It had one

Chapter XII

unexpected result: people became more angry than frightened and their determination to carry on was strengthened. Raids on Portsmouth became so frequent that few people ever went to shelter, but on 10 January 1941 there came a night when the whole city rocked with explosions. The noise of the planes started about 8 o'clock. They came in waves. First, hundreds of incendiaries were scattered, causing scores of fires until the whole city was alight. Then came the heavy bombers with the sickening noise of throbbing engines and, despite the fact that the city was brighter than it had ever been before, even in the heyday of peace, and the legitimate targets were plainly visible, the bombing was criminally inaccurate. Fire parties were doing sterling work, but the job was colossal. The fire-watchers in the Royal Sailors' Rest dealt successfully with the incendiaries which fell on the building but, when those that fell on neighbouring premises ignited in ever increasing numbers and caused an inferno of fire fanned by a strong north east wind to sweep uncontrollably down toward the Rest, it was time for all to take shelter, and only just in time. In a few hours the enormous building lay a heap of blackened ruins, tottering walls and twisted iron work, but not one man among the hundreds who had been at the Rest that night had been hurt.

The only part of the Rest complex which was at all usable was the lower floor of the office block which had been erected as a memorial to Sophia Wintz and was separated from the main block by a narrow street. The very next night there was on the site a mobile canteen ready and waiting to serve the men, and within six weeks new premises had been opened at Northleigh at the northern end of the city.

Three months later the Plymouth Rest was to suffer a similar annihilation. Plymouth had suffered cruelly from bombing and has been described as one of the worst blitzed cities in Europe. There had been more than 600 alerts and 59 heavy raids in which more than a thousand civilians had been killed and 3,200 injured. But the night of 22 April was one that those who suffered it will never forget. 'All hell was let loose', they say, and H.P. Twyford wrote, 'It came to our very door'. The raid took the usual pattern—first the city was drenched with incendiaries, then came the blast. Bombers came in droves; there was no 'let-up'. They seemed to bomb in rage; whole families were wiped out. Never had a night seemed so interminable.

In the Fore Street Rest over a thousand men had booked in for the night, but when the city became a wall of fire everyone was urged to seek shelter. This was difficult as so many of the shelters were also alight. The building was completely evacuated except for the cashier, a very little but very determined lady, who felt duty bound to guard the till, evidently with her life if necessary, but she was at last persuaded and led, still protesting, from the Rest. One of the staff ran and ran, looking for somewhere to shelter, and at last found herself on the shore where she took refuge under an upturned boat and lived to tell her tale. In the morning the staff returned to find only the shell of the building they had known for so long. One lady had to be restrained from going into the building to search for the mementos given by Miss Weston to the Rest. In all the misery cause by the raids there were gleams of humour to be found, and one was when the Rest was being demolished it was seen that eggs fried and placed between plates, then stacked in piles had not, on that fateful night, with all the rumbling, been moved an inch!

After the initial shock the Devonport staff soon got to work to find a substitute building. They took possession of a very old, disused, recruiting hut, which they first had to scrub over and over again before they could even think of preparing food there. Soon a canteen was established. As in Portsmouth the night following the dreadful raid, a mobile canteen was set up as near the ruins of the Rest as possible, with 'Service as usual'; another mobile canteen went regularly to the gun-sites and search-light bases on Dartmoor, its popularity was enormous as it carried home-made cakes and pies and could have sold ten times the number if rationing had made this possible.

The following year the small temporary Rest in Gosport also suffered damage. The residents were asleep at the time, but despite plaster falling off the ceilings, doors and windows blown in, beds covered with debris and splintered glass, as in Portsmouth and Plymouth there was not a single casualty.

After the war was over and Britain, with her allies, had done what she set out to do—to defeat Nazism—the mood of the country was not the same. Britain had taken much and was not going back to the old days of depression, the dole and the bread

Chapter XII

line. An election was held immediately after the peace, and the new Government, despite the desperate economic position of the country, introduced a vast welfare plan based on the Beveridge Report which, in many ways, was but an extension of the earlier work for the benefit of sailors, their wives and families introduced by Dame Agnes Weston and her helpers years before.

The Trustees of the Rests had to consider carefully their post-war programme and whether there was any need for Sailors' Rests in a country in which the naval forces, because of their specialisation, would be small. The Trustees decided that there would be, that men and women of the Navy would still need not only food and accommodation but also the spiritual guidance which the Rests could so amply provide. As Agnes had said many years before, 'I didn't leave a comfortable private life to open Sailors' Clubs, I wanted to open for tne men much more than that—Christian Homes'.

Having made their decision to carry on, large-scale rebuilding plans had to be instigated as urgently as possible—no easy matter in the immediate post-war atmosphere of material deficiency. It is noteworthy that within twelve years of the cessation of hostilities, not only had the major Rests been restored, but several new ones were in operation.

In 1952, a new Portsmouth Rest was re-opened on a site only a few hundred yards away from where the first one had stood. It later became possible to buy the Duchess of Albany Home which is situated in an ideally central position in Edinburgh Road, en route from the Dockyard to Commercial Road.

In 1957, a Rest was opened in Londonderry with accommodation for 46 men, the first in Ireland.

A huge modern Rest was opened in Devonport in 1959, which can accommodate 284 men and women, a wing of this building being set apart for members of the W.R.N.S. and commonly called 'The Wrenery'. Some of the cabins are fitted out as double bedrooms to cater for man and wife; in addition the very popular idea of the self-contained bed-sitting room was continued. As in other Rests, the restaurant is open to the general public, as years earlier Dame Agnes Weston had decreed should be the case. In the Devonport restaurant the dominant decoration is an historical and colourful seascape featuring Plymouth Sound painted by

R. Winston Sparrow, A.I.A.A.;while the murals in the restaurant of the Portsmouth Rest depict scenes from the more popular novels of Dickens. The new Rests are equipped with 20th-century comfort: television rooms, lounges, drying and ironing rooms, enormous billiard rooms, quiet rooms for contemplation and devotion, and large halls for meetings, films, concerts and services.

The most recent Rest, at least in the United Kingdom, was opened at Weymouth when an old public house *The Lamb and Flag* in Lower Bond Street was bought and converted into a new Sailors' Rest and modern naval meeting centre. It is interesting to note that the transformation of a public house to a temperance home has been repeated as in the case of the earlier Rests at both Plymouth and Portsmouth. Private houses too have been bought and turned into flats for naval families and are very popular, especially with young married couples who are not in one place long enough to qualify for a council house. These flats are certainly a far cry from the married quarters of an earlier age.

Quite apart from these residential concerns, two centres for Christian work have been set up at Rowner, Gosport and St. Budeaux, Plymouth—these are, in effect, Christian social and welfare centres where the Missioners-in-charge are always available to give spiritual and material guidance to naval families.

The good that the Missioners attached to the Rests do is immeasurable. They are usually ex-naval men dedicated to Christian work whose aim is to help men and women in the Royal Navy. They meet incoming ships and their 'open sesame' to conversation with the crew is the magazine *Ashore and Afloat*, with its modern presentation of Naval news and the Gospel message.

Although the days of the vast Navy have passed, the work of the Royal Sailors' Rest is still spreading. This is illustrated by the opening of the first overseas Rest at Singapore. The idea was mooted by Admiral Sir David Luce when he was Commander-in-Chief Far East and was approved by the Trustees. Building commenced in January 1963 and was completed in nine months—a first class Rest with 72 bedrooms (two-thirds of them air-conditioned), lounges, games rooms and a magnificent swimming pool, all finished in so short a time, waiting to welcome the naval personnel. The opening ceremony was performed by Admiral Sir

Chapter XII

Desmond Dreyer, K.C.B., C.B.E., D.S.C. and was a very gay affair with the Royal Marines' Band playing to entertain the three hundred guests present, and this in spite of a fire which broke out on the eve of the ceremony. Quick and strenuous action soon made good the damage done, but the fire revealed signs that the site had once been a Japanese stronghold during the island's occupation; today there stands on this same site a Christian Rest.

This is the story of a woman who, with the loyal help of a true friend, a century ago took upon herself to minister and protect a section of Victorian society which was then despised and rejected—the 'common' blue-jacket, of whom even the understanding Reverend J. Wesley said, 'I doubt if any heathen sailor in any country or age ever comes up to ours for profound ignorance and bare-faced shocking impiety'. It tells of the hard struggle these women waged, and of their ultimate victory over intolerance and prejudice, so that the lower deck rating of the Royal Navy today enjoys his proper status in society.

Throughout the arduous years of their toil they were constantly sustained by their innate love of Christ and His teachings, the foremost of which is 'Love thy neighbour'.

BIBLIOGRAPHY

BERESFORD, Admiral Lord Charles,	*Memoirs,* London, 1914
CHAPPELL, J.	*Four Noble Women and their Work,* London, 1898
	Agnes Weston, the Sailors' Friend London, 1935
	They who Comforted, London
CLOWES, Sir William L.	*The Royal Navy – A History from the Earliest Times to the Present,* London, 1897–1903
DOLLING, R.W.R.,	*Ten Years in a Portsmouth Slum,* London, 1896
DORLING, H.T.,	*Men O'War* (Lord Charles Beresford), London, 1929
GATES, W.G.,	*Portsmouth in the Past,* Portsmouth, 1926
JARRETT, D.,	*British Naval Dress,* London, 1960
LEWIS, M.A.,	*The Navy in Transition, 1814–1864,* London, 1965
MAUD, C.E.,	*Sparks among the Stubble* (Agnes Weston), London, 1924
OSBORNE, REV. C.E.,	*The Life of Father Dolling,* London, 1903
STEEVENS, G.W.,	*From Capetown to Ladysmith,* London, 1900
TOMKINSON, E.M.,	*Agnes Weston* (in *The World's Workers*), London, 1885.
TREVELYAN, G.M.,	*A Shortened History of England,* (Penguin), London, 1942
TWYFORD, H.P.,	*It Came to our Door. Plymouth in the World War,* Plymouth, 1946.
VERNEY, Sir Edmund H., Bt.,	*The Last Four Days of the Eurydice,* Portsmouth, 1878.

WARNER, O.,	*The Navy,* (Penguin), London, 1968
WESTON, Dame Agnes	*My Life Among the Blue Jackets,* London, 1909.
—	*England Home and Duty,* London
WINTZ, Dame Sophia	*Our Blue Jackets. Miss Weston's Life and Work among our Sailors,* London, 1890.

ADDITIONAL MATERIAL

Ashore and Afloat 1899–1967
Annual Reports of the Royal Sailors' Rests. 1910–1960
Admiralty Minutes on the loss of H.M.S. *Victoria.* By Command of Her Majesty—November 1893—printed by H.M. Stationery Office
Mariners' Mirror 1963–1968
Letter, Memoirs and Diary—Lent by Mrs. C.H. Weston.

INDEX

NOTE: As references to Agnes Weston, Sophia Wintz, the Royal Navy and blue-jackets abound in this book, no entries for them are given in this index.

Abbey Church, Bath: 10
Accident to Agnes Weston: 120
Alberta, Royal yacht: 135
Alexandra, Queen: 135
Alexandria, Egypt: 95
Alfred, King: 67
Alliance: 113
American sailors entertain Miss Weston: 113
Ancestry of Agnes Weston: 6, 7
Ancestry of Sophia Wintz: 19
Antagonism of Devonport publicans: 46
Arabi, Mr. (the teapot): 36
Arabi, Pasha: 95, 96
Ashore and Afloat: 24, 35, 74, 100, 107, 112 - 114, 124, 125, 128, 135, 137, 145, 147, 148
Aunt Mary: 127
Aunt Susan: 127

Ballard, Miss: 109
Band of H.M.S. *Excellent:* 109
Bath: 3, 4, 8, 10, 14, 16, 18, 23, 30, 104
Bath, United Hospital: 13
Bayly, Anne (maternal grandmother): 2, 3
Bayly, Robert (maternal grandfather): 2
Beresford Block: 59
Beresford, Charles: 49, 52, 95, 96
Bishop of St. Albans: 123
Bishop of Chichester: 123
Blue-backs: 18
Boer War: 95
Bogatyr: 118
Bombing of Rests: 149, 150
Boys' Naval Brigade: 76
Brittania: 22, 43
British Empire: 93
Brown, George (formerly Dowkonott): 16, 17, 33

Caine, W.S. (M.P. – Civil Lord of Admiralty): 49

Cambridge Settlement: 104
Camoerdown: 85
Cape Trece: 79
Carpenter, Boyd (Captain R.N.): 86
Catherine II, Empress of Russia: 116
Cesarevitch: 118
Charity organisation Society: 104
Charlotte Street, Portsmouth: 53, 54
Chartered Patriotic Society: 88
Chatham: 34
Cholera, in Portsmouth: 61
Christian Union: 97
Christian, The (periodical): 40
Christmas parties: 75
Christmas presents for Naval Brigade: 100
Church Assembly at Brighton and Portsmouth: 123
Clifton: 23
Clubs for wives of naval men: 72
Commercial Road, Portsmouth: 54 - 56, 151
Co-op. Shop, Devonport: 39, 41, 55, 122
Coronation of King Edward VII: 108
Coronation of King George V: 118
Court of Inquiry on loss of *Serpent:* 82
Court of Inquiry on loss of *Victoria:* 85
Cowell, Sir John: 86
Crimea, The: 66
Crimean veterans: 87
Crimean war: 93, 94
Crocodile: 17, 33
Crown Princess of Germany: 131, 132
Currey, Mrs. Bernard: 147, 148

Daily Mail, report on visit of French ships: 116
Dardanelles: 140
Denny, Anthony: 56
Depot opened for mourning at Portsmouth Rest: 87
Devil's Acre, Portsea: 54
Devonport: 1, 18, 25, 31, 41, 45, 55

Index

Devonport Rest: 40, 43 - 46, 47, 49, 55, 125
Diamond Jubilee Block: 59, 132
Dickens, Charles: 28, 137
Discovery: 18
Dixon, Rev. A.L.: 14
Dock Gates Inn: 47
Dolling, Father: 62, 78, 88, 89

Earthquake at Messina: 90, 91
Edinburgh, Duke of (also Saxe Coburg & Gotha): 19, 80, 133, 134
Edward VII, King: 25, 108, 125
Egyptian War: 36, 95
Emden: 127
Employment bureau: 77
Ensleigh (Bath): 10, 12, 13, 18, 104
Ensleigh (Grayshott): 137
Eurydice: 51, 52, 79, 86
Evans of the *Broke:* 125

First Sailors Rest: 42
First suggestion of a Sailors Rest: 38
First World War: 29, 37, 95, 100, 112, 116, 118, 125
Fleming, Rev. James: 8, 9, 12
Flogging in the Royal Navy: 65
Flynn, Rev. Dr.: 142
French Maid, The (public house): 59
Foudroyant: 24
Fund for dependants of victims of *Victoria* disaster: 87
Funeral of Agnes Weston: 142
Funeral of Sophia Wintz: 146

German Sailors' Home: 101
Gifts from Japanese sailors: 109
Gifts from Russian sailors: 117
Gloucester Cathedral: 11
Grant, H.G. – Admiral C.B.: 48
Graspan, Battle of: 99
Grayshott: 136
Greenwich fund: 80
Greenwich pensions: 80
Grid iron roll, The – naval manoeuvre: 84
Grog (rum): 27, 35
Grog shop: 29
Grog tub: 34

Half-pay day: 75
Hamoaze: 24, 141
Hare, Mrs. Marcus: 51, 52
Hare, Marcus – Captain R.N.: 81

Harris, Rear Admiral: 98
Haslar Hospital: 34
Hartford: 113
Head, Canon: 40
Hecla: 94
Hohenzollern, German Royal yacht: 112
Holiday home, Saltash: 73
Hood: 79

Implacable: 24
Impregnable: 113
Inconstant: 37
Indian Mutiny: 94
Inguin, Gore – Japanese Admiral: 108
Inn signs (with naval connotations): 28

Jellicoe, Commander (later Admiral of the Fleet): 85
John, King: 54
Jones, Admiral Sir Lewis

Kaiser and Kaiserin of Germany: 112
Kashima: 109
Katori: 109, 110
Keyham: 51
King-Hall, Admiral Sir William: 31
Kitting-up: 78, 102
Knowles, W.G. – Able Seaman of the *Brok* 126

Ladysmith, Siege of: 98
Lanyon, Mrs.: 85
Lansdown: 4, 124
Lansdown Hill: 9
Last Annual Report by Sophia Wintz: 145
Letters, first beginnings: 16, 17
Life among the blue-jackets (book): 44
Lion: 24
Liverpool Medical Mission: 33
Londonerry Rest opened: 151
Lucas, Charles: 94
Lucknow: 94

Malvern: 104
Manning Committee: 65
Manning Reports: 68
Marine buglers: 101
Markham, Rear Admiral: 85
Marseillaise: 115
Marsh, Catherine: 13, 14
Memorial window: 141, 142
Messages of sympathy on death of Agnes

Index

Weston: 143
Messages of sympathy on death of Sophia Wintz: 146
Minerva: 91

National disaster fund at Rests: 82
National Temperance League: 30, 34, 52, 55
Napier, Admiral: 94
Napier's Inn: 47
Naval Brigade: 37, 94 - 96, 100
Naval scrapbook: 85
Naval welfare: 51
Nelson, Lord: 67, 110

Obelisk Fields, Devonport: 75
Olga: 118

Paxton, Sir Joseph: 10
Phillips, Arthur: 26
Pinney, Colonel: 15
Pledges – Signing the: 33
Plymouth: 10, 18, 23, 24, 44, 79, 111
Pompey (nickname for Portsmouth): 124
Portland: 24
Portsmouth: 1, 16, 18, 33, 34, 51, 53, 55, 75, 79
Portsmouth Rest opened: 57, 58
Powerful: 97, 98, 100
Pressgang: 64, 65
Professional letter writers: 17
Profits from Naval Exhibition: 133

Queen Victoria's Memorial Hall: 49
Queen Street, Portsea: 54, 58

Recall day: 75
Reindeer: 30
Robinson, Sarah: 53, 54
Royal Commission at Devonport (under Lord Farrer): 75
Royal Naval Christian Union: 74
Royal Naval Exhibition (1892): 133
Royal Navy Rendezvous (public house): 47
Royal Naval Temperance Society: 37, 38, 74
Royal Sailors' Rest Needlework Guild: 73
Royal Warrant for the Sailors' Rests: 134

Savage, F.M. – Lt. Cdr. R.N.: 148
Schoole of Cookery, South Kensington: 41
Second World War: 25, 148 - 153
Serpent: 79, 80 - 82, 133,
Singapore Rest opened: 152

Sion Place, Bath: 49
Slava: 118
Sleipner: 112
Somerset Militia: 14
Somerset, Lady Henry: 123
Somerset Place: 5
South Africa: 96, 99
Southampton: 97
Sparrow, R. Winston, A.I.A.A.: 152
Spithead: 67, 100
Steevens, G.W.: 98
Stephens, Frank: 30
Stoke: 38
Suryalus: 91
Switzerland: 20, 21
Sydney: 127

Temple Combe: 23, 24
Ten Years in the Slums (book): 88
Terrible: 97, 98
Thalia: 34
Topaze: 33
Trinity College, Cambridge: 43
Trotter, Mr. de – Naval surgeon: 64
Tryon, Admiral Sir George, K.C.B.: 84, 85
Turny, Richard: 31

Underneath the Searchlight (book): 110

Vernon, Admiral (Old Grog): 27
Vernon: 27
Victor Emanuel, King of Italy: 91
Victoria: 84, 85, 86, 88 - 90
Victoria fund: 90
Victoria Jubilee Nursing Association: 73
Victoria, Queen: 3, 27, 108, 131, 134, 135, 136
Victory: 110
Visit of American ships: 112 - 114
Visit of French ships: 110, 114 - 116
Visit of German ships: 111, 112
Visit of Japanese ships: 108, 109, 110
Visit of Russian ships: 116 - 118
von Koester, Admiral of German Navy: 111

Waterlooville: 104
Wesley, Dr.: 11, 12
Western Mercury, interview with Miss Weston: 101
Weston, Agnes – mother (nee Bayley): 3, 5, 6, 9, 10, 30, 104
Weston, Charles – father: 1, 2, 3, 4, 5, 6, 9,

Index

10, 12, 19, 34
Weston, Charles – brother: 3
Weston, Charles – nephew: 104, 145 - 148
Weston, Charles – cousin: 94
Weston, Emily – sister: 3, 16, 30, 53, 130
Weston, Gould Hunter – cousin: 94, 95
Weston, John – nephew: 104 - 107
Weston, Samuel – paternal grandfather: 1

Weymouth: 1
Weymouth Rest opened: 152
Williams, Miss: 30
Wilson, Captain R.N., V.C.: 32
Wintz, Mrs (Frau): 20 - 22, 25, 26, 78
Wintzenaue Castle: 20
Women at War: 126
Wren, Arthur: 41